Bibliographies for Biblical Research

Old Testament Series
in Twenty-Two Volumes

General Editor

Watson E. Mills

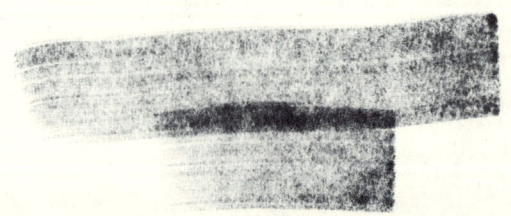

Bibliographies for Biblical Research

Old Testament Series
in Twenty-Two Volumes

Volume XIII

The Book of Job

Compiled by

Thomas F. Dailey

MELLEN BIBLICAL PRESS
Lewiston/Queenston/Lampeter

Library of Congress Cataloging-in-Publication Data

This book has been registered with the Library of Congress.

ISBN 0-7734-2437-7   (hard)

```
This is volume 13 in the continuing series
Bibliographies for Biblical Research
Old Testament Series
Volume 13   ISBN 0-7734-2437-7
Series 0-7734-9426-X
```

A CIP catalog record for this book is available from the British Library.

Copyright © 1997 The Edwin Mellen Press

All rights reserved. For information contact

    The Edwin Mellen Press   The Edwin Mellen Press
    Box 450   Box 67
    Lewiston, New York   Queenston, Ontario
    USA 14092-0450   CANADA L0S 1L0

                The Edwin Mellen Press, Ltd.
                Lampeter, Dyfed, Wales
              UNITED KINGDOM SA48 7DY

Printed in the United States of America

Dedication

to

Rev. Prof. Dermot Cox, o.f.m. (†)

whose scholarship has led many
in the pursuit of wisdom

CONTENTS

Introduction to the Series ix

Preface xi

Abbreviations xiii

Part One — Citations by TEXT 1

Part Two — Citations by SUBJECT 51

Part Three — GENERAL Citations 121

AUTHOR Index 139

Introduction to the Series

This volume is one in a series of bibliographies on the books of the Hebrew and Christian Bibles as well as the deutero-canonicals. This ambitious series calls for some 35-40 volumes over the next 3-5 years compiled by practicing scholars from various traditions.

Each author (compiler) of these volumes is working within the general framework adopted for the series, i.e., citations are to works published within the twentieth century that make important contributions to the understanding of the text and backgrounds of the various books.

Obviously the former criterion is more easily quantifiable than the latter, and it is precisely at this point that an individual compiler makes her/his specific contribution. We are not intending to be comprehensive in the sense of definitive, but where resources are available, as many listings as possible have been included.

The arrangement for the entries, in most volumes in the series, consists of three divisions: scriptural citations; subject citations; commentaries. In some cases the first two categories may duplicate each other to some degree. Multiple citations by scriptural citation are also included where relevant.

Those who utilize these volumes are invited to assist the compilers by noting textual errors as well as obvious omissions that ought to be taken into account in subsequent printings. Perfection is nowhere more elusive than in the citation of bibliographic materials. We would welcome your assistance at this point.

When the series is completed, the entire contents of all volumes (updated) will be available on CD-ROM. This option will be available, without charge, to those who have subscribed to the casebound volumes.

We hope that these bibliographies will contribute to the discussions and research going on in the field among faculty as well as students. They should serve a significant role as reference works in both research and public libraries.

I wish to thank the staff and editors of the Edwin Mellen Press, and especially Professor Herbert Richardson, for the gracious support of this series.

Watson E. Mills, Series Editor
Mercer University
Macon GA 31207
December 1997

Preface

This bibliography on the Book of Job provides a listing of works published in the twentieth century through mid-1997. These works include books and monographs, journal articles, essays in collected works, and dissertations related to the biblical book.

Though no extant bibliography on the Book of Job currently exists, some larger commentaries include many helpful citations: Jean Lévêque, *Job et son Dieu: Essai d'exégèse et de théologie biblique*, 2 volumes (Gabalda, 1970); Norman Habel, *The Book of Job: A Commentary* (Westminster Press, 1985); David J.A. Clines, *Job 1-20* (Word Books, 1989). The most thorough compilation of sources can be culled from the *Elenchus of Biblica* (Biblical Institute Press), but this reference is only completed through 1992.

Creating a work such as this is, indeed, a time-consuming and tedious task. For their help in this effort, I would like to express my gratitude to Watson E. Mills (editor of this series), whose patience has been encouraging. And I would also like to acknowledge the invaluable and generous assistance of two of my students: Lilian Figueroa began this project with me, and Nathan Cromly has helped bring it to completion. Their work may have often seemed thankless to them, but to me it is certainly appreciated.

It is my hope that this work may contribute in some, small way to the research of others, as they continue to probe the depths of this classic biblical tale.

Thomas F. Dailey
Allentown College of St. Francis de Sales
Center Valley, PA 18034
August 1997

Abbreviations

AAR	American Academy of Religion
ABD	D.N. Freedman et al. (eds.)., *Anchor Bible Dictionary*
AGJU	Arbeiten zur Geschichte des antiken Judentums und des Urchristentums
AJBA	*Australian Journal of Biblical Archaeology*
AJSL	*American Journal of Semitic Languages and Literatures*
ALUOS	*Annual of Leeds University Oriental Society*
Ang	*Angelicum*
AnGreg	Analecta Gregoriania
Anton	*Antonianum*
ATD	Das Alte Testament Deutsch
ATR	*Anglican Theological Review*
Aug	*Augustinianum*
BeO	*Bibbia e oriente*
BETL	Bibliotheca ephemeridum theologicarum lovaniensium
Bib	*Biblica*
BibOr	Biblica et orientalis
BIES	*Bulletin of the Israel Exploration Society*
Bijdr	*Bijdragen*
BJRL	*Bulletin of the John Rylands University Library of Manchester*
BJS	Brown Judaic Studies
BK	*Bibel und Kirche*
BLit	*Bible und Liturgie*
BN	*Biblische Notizien*
BRev	*Bible Review*
BR	*Biblical Research*
BSac	*Bibliotheca Sacra*
BT	*Bible Translator*
BTB	*Biblical Theology Bulletin*

BurH	*Buried History*
BZ	*Biblische Zeitschrift*
BZAW	Beheifte zur *ZAW*
CAT	*Commentaire de l'Ancien Testament*
CBQ	*Catholic Biblical Quarterly*
CBQMS	*CBQ* Monograph Studies
CH	*Church History*
CJT	*Canadian Journal of Theology*
ConBOT	*Coniectanea biblica, Old Testament*
CQ	*Church Quarterly*
EBib	Études bibliques
EncJud	*Encyclopedia Judaica*
ErFor	Erträge der Forschung
EstBib	*Estudios bíblicos*
EvQ	*Evangelical Quarterly*
EvT	*Evangelische Theologie*
ExpTim	*Expository Times*
FRLANT	Forschungen zur Religion und Literatur des Alten und Neuen testaments
Greg	*Gregorianum*
HAR	*Hebrew Annual Review*
HerTS	*Hervormde Teologiese Studies*
HeyJ	*Heythrop Journal*
HTR	*Harvard Theological Review*
HTS	Harvard Theological Studies
HUCA	*Hebrew Union College Annual*
IBC	Interpretation: A Bible Commentary for Teaching and Preaching
ICC	International Critical Commentary
IDB	G.A. Buttrick (ed.). *Interpreter's Dictionary of the Bible*
IDBSup	Supplementary Volume to *IDB*

Int	*Interpretation*
ITQ	*Irish Theological Quarterly*
JAAR	*Journal of the American Academy of Religion*
JANES	*Journal of the Ancient Near Eastern Society*
JAOS	*Journal of the American Oriental Society*
JBL	*Journal of Biblical Literature*
JBQ	*Jewish Biblical Quarterly*
JBR	*Journal of Bible and Religion*
JEOL	*Jaarbericht ... ex oriente lux*
JETS	*Journal of the Evangelical Theological Society*
JJS	*Journal of Jewish Studies*
JNES	*Journal of Near Eastern Studies*
JNSL	*Journal of Northwest Semitic Languages*
JQR	*Jewish Quarterly Review*
JR	*Journal of Religion*
JSHRZ	*Jüdische Schriften aus hellenistisch-römanischer Zeit*
JSJ	*Journal for the Study of Judaism in the Persian, Hellenistic, and Roman Periods*
JSOT	*Journal for the Study of the Old Testament*
JSOTSup	JSOT Supplement Series
JSP	*Journal for the Study of the Pseudepigrapha*
JSS	*Journal of Semitic Studies*
JTS	*Journal of Theological Studies*
KAT	E. Semmin (ed.)., Kommentar zum A.T.
KD	*Kerygma und Dogma*
LD	Lectio divina
LTP	*Laval théologique et philosophique*
LumVie	*Lumière et vie*

MScRel	*Mélanges de science religieuse*
MTZ	*Münchener theologische Zeitschrift*
NBl	*New Blackfriars*
NCB	New Century Bible
NCE	M.R.P. McGuire et al. (eds.)., *New Catholic Encyclopedia*
NedTTs	*Nederlands theologisch tijdschrift*
NICOT	New International Commentary on the Old Testament
NJBC	R.E. Brown et al. (eds.)., *New Jerome Biblical Commentary*
NRT	*Nouvelle revue théologique*
OBO	Orbis biblicus et orientalis
Or	*Orientalia*
OrChr	*Oriens christianus*
OTE	Old Testament Essays
OTL	Old Testament Library
OTM	Old Testament Message
OTS	Oudtestamentische studiën
PAAJR	*Proceedings of the American Academy of Jewish Research*
PEGLMBS	*Proceedings of the Eastern Great Lakes and Midwest Biblical Societies*
PEQ	*Palestine Exploration Quarterly*
PIBA	*Proceedings of the Irish Biblical Association*
PSB	*Princeton Seminary Bulletin*
QD	Wuaestiones disputatae
RB	*Revue biblique*
RCB	*Revista de cultura bíblica*
REJ	*Revue des études juives*
ResQ	*Restoration Quarterly*
RevExp	*Review and Expositor*
RevistB	*Revista bíblica*
RevQ	*Revue de Qumran*

RHPR	Revie d'historie et de philosophie religieuses
RHR	Revue de l'historie des religions
RivB	Rivista biblica
RTL	Revue théologique de Louvain
SBFLA	Studii biblici franciscani liber annuus
SBL	Society of Biblical Literature
SBLDS	SBL Disseration Series
SBLSBS	SBL, Sources for Biblical Study
SBLSCS	SBL, Septuagint and Cognate Studies
SBLSP	SBL Seminar Papers
SBT	Studies in Biblical Theology
ScEs	Science et esprit
ScrB	Scripture Bulletin
SEÅ	Svensk exegetisk årsbok
Sef	Sefarad
SJT	Scottish Joural of Theology
SKKNT	Stutttgarter kleiner Kommentar, Neues Testament
SNTSMS	Society for New Testament Studies Monograph Series
SR	Studies in Religion/Sciences religieuses
STK	Svensk teologisk Kvartalskrift
SWJT	Southwestern Journal of Theology
TBT	The Bible Today
ThStud	Theologische Studiën
TLZ	Theologische Literaturzeitung
TRE	Theologische Realenzklopädie
TTKi	Tidsskrift for teologi og kirke
TToday	Theology Today
TTZ	Trierer theologische Zeitschrift
TynOTC	Tyndale Old Testament Commentaries
TZ	Theologische Zeitschrift
UF	Ugarit-Forschungen
USQR	Union Seminary Quarterly Review

VSpir	*Vie spirituelle*
VT	*Vetus Testamentum*
WBC	Word Biblical Commentary
WD	*Wort und Dienst*
WO	*Welt des Orients*
WTJ	*Westminster Theological Journal*
ZAW	*Zeitschrift für die alttestamentliche Wissenschaft*
ZDMG	*Zeitschrift der deutschen morgenländischen Gesellschaft*
ZNW	*Zeitschrift für die neutestamentliche Wissenschaft*
ZRGG	*Zeitschrift für Religions- und Geistesgeschichte*
ZTK	*Zeitschrift für Theologie und Kirche*

Part One

Citations by TEXT

<u>Framework</u> (1:1-2:10 and 42:7-17)

<u>Prologue</u>
- chapter 1
- chapter 2

<u>Dialogues</u>

- Opening soliloquy (chap. 3)

- First cycle of speeches (chaps. 4-14)
  - Eliphaz (4-5)
  - Job (6-7)
  - Bildad (8)
  - Job (9-10)
  - Zophar (11)
  - Job (12-14)

- Second cycle of speeches (chaps. 15-21)
  - Eliphaz (15)
  - Job (16-17)
  - Bildad (18)
  - Job (19)
  - Zophar (20)
  - Job (21)

- Third cycle of speeches (chaps. 22-27)
  - Eliphaz (22)
  - Job (23-24)
  - ??? (25-27)

- Poem on Wisdom (chap. 28)

- Closing soliloquy (chaps. 29-31)
  - chapter 29
  - chapter 30
  - chapter 31

speeches of <u>Elihu</u>
- chapter 32
- chapter 33
- chapter 34
- chapter 35
- chapter 36
- chapter 37

<u>Theologue</u>

- First speech of Yahweh (38-39)
- Job's first response (40:1-5)

- Second speech of Yahweh (40:6 -41:34)
- Job's second response (42:1-6)

<u>Epilogue</u> (42:7-17)

FRAMEWORK (1:1-2:10 and 42:7-17)

0001 Kautzsch, K. *Das sogenannte Volksbuch von Hiob und der Ursprung von Hiob I, II, XLII,7-17: Ein Beitrag nach der Integrität des Buches Hiob.* Tübingen: J.C.B. Mohr, 1900.

0002 Owens, J.J. "The Prologue and the Epilogue." *RevExp* 68/4 (1971): 457-467.

0003 Hurvitz, A. "The Date of the Prose-Tale of Job Linguistically Reconsidered." *HTR* 67 (1974): 17-34.

0004 Polzin, Robert. "The Framework of the Book of Job." *Int* 28 (1974): 182-200.

0005 Müller, Hans-Peter. "Die weisheitliche Lehrerzählung im Alten Testament und seiner Umwelt." *WO* 9 (1977): 77-98.

0006 Hoffman, Rudolf. "Eine Parallele zur Rahmenerzählung des Buches Hiob in I Chr 7, 20-29?" *ZAW* 92 (1980): 120-132.

0007 Weimar, P. "Literarkritisches zur Ijobnovelle." *BN* 12 (1980): 62-80.

0008 Cooper, A. "Narrative Theory and the Book of Job." *SR* 11 (1982): 35-44.

0009 Maag, V. *Hiob: Wandlung und Verarbeitung des Problems in Novelle, Dialogdichtung, und Spätfassungen* [FRLANT, 128]. Göttingen: Vandenhoeck & Ruprecht, 1982, pp. 20-90.

0010 Clines, D.J.A. "In Search of the Indian Job." *VT* 33 (1983): 398-418.

0011 Fohrer, Georg. "Überlieferung und Wandlung der Hioblegende." In *Studien zum Buche Hiob, 1956-1979* [BZAW, 159]. Berlin: de Gruyter, 1983, pp. 37-59.

0012 Brenner, Athalya. "'Job the Pious': The Characterization of Job in the Narrative Framework of the Book." *JSOT* 43 (1989): 37-52.

0013 Erikson, Gösta and Kristina Jonasson. "Jobsbokens juridiska grundmönster." *STK* 65/2 (1989): 64-69.

0014 Schwienhorst-Schönberger, Ludger and Georg Steins. "Zur Entstehung, Gestalt und Bedeutung der Ijob-Erzählung (Ijob 1f; 42)." *BZ* 33 (1989): 1-24.

0015 Coogan, Michael D. "Job's Children." In Tzvi Abusch, et al (eds.). *Lingering over Words: Studies in Ancient Near East Literature* [festschrift for W.L. Moran; HSS, 37]. Atlanta: Scholars Press, 1990, pp. 135-147.

0016 Oosthuizen, M.J. "Divine Insecurity and Joban Heroism: A Reading of the Narrative Framework of Job." *OTE* 4 (1991): 295-315.

0017 Nielsen, Kirsten. "Whatever Became of You, Satan? or, A Literary-Critical Analysis of the Role of Satan in the Book of Job." In Klaus-Dietrich Schunck and Augustin Mathias (eds.). *Goldene Äpfel in silbernen Schalen* [XIII Congress of the IOSOT]. Frankfurt: Lang, 1992, pp. 129-134.

0018 Berges, Ulrich. "Der Ijobrahmen (Ijob 1,1-2,10; 42,7-17): Theologische Versuche angesichts unschuldigen Leidens." *BZ* 39 (1995): 225-245.

PROLOGUE (chapters 1-2)

0019 Rongy, H. "Le prologue de livre de Job." *Revue Ecclésiastique de Liège* 25 (1933): 168-171.

0020 Gordis, Robert. "The Temptation of Job — Tradition versus Experience in Religion." *Judaism* 4 (1955): 195-208.

0021 Sarna, N.M. "Epic Substratum in the Prose of Job." *JBL* 76 (1957): 13-25.

0022 Rao, S. Prabhakara and M. Reddy. "Job and His Satan - Parallels in Indian Scripture." *ZAW* 91 (1979): 416-422.

0023 Görg, M. "Ijob aus dem Lande 'Ūs: Ein Beitrag zur 'theologischen Geographie'." *BN* 12 (1980): 7-12.

0024 Weiss, Meir. *The Story of Job's Beginning, Job 1-2: A Literary Analysis.* Jerusalem: Magnes Press, 1983.

0025 Clines, David J.A. "False Naivety in the Prologue to Job." *HAR* 9 (1985): 127-136.

0026 Michel, Walter L. *Job in the Light of Northwest Semitic,* vol I: Prologue and First Cycle of Speeches (Job 1:1 — 14:22) [BibOr, 42]. Rome: Pontifical Biblical Institute, 1987.

0027 Meier, Sam. "Job i-ii: A Reflection of Genesis i-iii." *VT* 39 (1989): 183-193.

0028 Cooper, Alan. "Reading and Misreading the Prologue to Job." *JSOT* 46 (1990): 67-79.

0029 Grayston, Kenneth. "Satan and Job." *ScrB* 23 (1993): 2-7.

0030 Handy, Lowell K. "The Authorization of Divine Power and the Guilt of God in the Book of Job: Useful Ugaritic Parallels." *JSOT* 60 (1993): 107-118.

0031 Fleming, Daniel E. "Job: The Tale of Patient Faith and the Book of God's Dilemma." *VT* 44/4 (1994): 468-482.

Prologue - Chapter 1

0032 Waldman, N.M. "Hebrew Oz and the Divine Aura." *Gratz College Jewish Studies* 1 (1972): 7-13.

0033 Owen, G. Frederick. "The Land of Uz." In Roy B. Zuck (ed.). *Sitting with Job: Selected Studies on the Book of Job.* Grand Rapids: Baker, 1992, pp. 245-247.

0034 Görg, Manfred. "Ijob aus dem Lande 'ûṣ: ein Beitrag zur 'theologischen Geographie'." *BN* 12 (1980): 7-12.

1:1-5

0035 Leloir, L. "Lectio divina: Job 1,1-5 sainteté juive et sainteté chrètienne." *Collectanea Cisterciensia* 32 (1970): 268-288.

1:3

0036 Rinaldi, G. "*mqnh (miqneh)*. Giobbe 1,3." *BeO* 20 (1978): 60.

1:5

0037 Jacob, B. "Erklärung einiger Hiob-Stellen: 1,5; 1,22; 2,4; 2,10." *ZAW* 31 (1912): 278-287.

0038 Joüon, P. "Notes philologiques sure le texte hébreu de Job 1,5; 9,35; 12,21; 28,1; 28,27; 29,14." *Bib* 11 (1930): 322-324.

1:18

0039 Barr, James. "Hebrew '*ad*, especially at Job 1.18 and Neh. vii.3." *JSS* 27/2 (1982): 177-192.

1:20-22

0040 Vogels, W. "Job's Empty Pious Slogans (Job 1,20-22; 2,8-10)." In W. Beuken (ed.). *The Book of Job* [BETL, 114]. Leuven: University Press, 1994, pp. 369-376.

0041 Vogels, Walter. "Job's Superficial Faith in His First Reactions to Suffering (Job 1:20-22; 2:8-10)." *Eglise et Théologie* 25 (1994): 343-339.

1:21

0042 Ricciotti, G. "Et nu j'y retournerai (Job 1:21)." *ZAW* 67 (1955): 249-251.

0042a Vall, Gregory. "The Enigma of Job 1,21a." *Bib* 76 (1995): 325-342.

1:22

0043 Jacob, B. "Erklärung einiger Hiob-Stellen: 1,5; 1,22; 2,4; 2,10." *ZAW* 31 (1912): 278-287.

Prologue - Chapter 2

2:4

    0044 Jacob, B. "Erklärung einiger Hiob-Stellen: 1,5; 1,22; 2,4; 2,10." *ZAW* 31 (1912): 278-287.

2:8-10

    0045 Vogels, W. "Job's Empty Pious Slogans (Job 1,20-22; 2,8-10)." In W. Beuken (ed.). *The Book of Job* [BETL, 114]. Leuven: University Press, 1994, pp. 369-376.

    0046 Vogels, Walter. "Job's Superficial Faith in His First Reactions to Suffering (Job 1:20-23; 2:8-10)." *Eglise et Théologie* 25 (1994): 343-339.

2:9

    0047 Rottenberg, M. "Did Job's Wife Really Use a Euphemism in Job 2:9?" *Le* 52 (1988): 176-177.

    0048 West, Gerald. "Hearing Job's Wife." *OTE* 4 (1991): 107-131.

    0048a Gitay, Zefira. "The Portrayal of Job's Wife and Her Representation in the Visual Arts." In Astrid B. Beck, et al (eds.). *Fortunate the Eyes That See* [festschrift for D.N. Freedman]. Grand Rapids: Eerdmans, 1995, pp. 516-526.

2:10

    0049 Jacob, B. "Erklärung einiger Hiob-Stellen: 1,5; 1,22; 2,4; 2,10." *ZAW* 31 (1912): 278-287.

2:12

    0050 Houtman, C. "Zu Hiob 2:12." *ZAW* 90 (1978): 269-272.

2:13

    0051 McCormick, S. "Someone HAD to Speak! A Sermon on Job 2:13." *Int* 20 (1966): 211-217.

DIALOGUES (chaps. 3-31)

0052 Kelley, P.H. "The Speeches of Job: the Three Friends." *RevExp* 68/4 (1971): 479-485.

0053 Williams, D.L. "The Speeches of Job." *RevExp* 68/4 (1971): 469-478.

0054 Urbrock, W.J. "Formula and Theme in the Song-Cycle of Job." *SBL Proceedings* 108/2 (1972): 459-487.

0055 Snaith, N.H. "The Introductions to the Speeches in the Book of Job. Are They in Prose or in Verse?" *Textus* 8 (1973): 133-137.

0056 Cox, Dermot. "Reason in Revolt: The Poetic Dialogues in the Book of Job." *SBFLA* 24 (1974): 317-328.

0057 Clines, David J.A. "The Arguments of Job's Three Friends." In David J.A. Clines, David M. Gunn, and Alan J. Hauser (eds.). *Art and Meaning: Rhetoric in Biblical Literature* [JSOTSup, 19]. Sheffield: Almond Press, 1982, pp. 199-214.

0058 Webster, E.C. "Strophic Patterns in Job 3-28." *JSOT* 26 (1983): 33-60.

0059 Cox, Dermot. "A Rational Inquiry into God: Chapters 4-27 of the Book of Job." *Greg* 67 (1986): 621-658.

0060 Wolfers, David. "The Speech-Cycles in the Book of Job." *VT* 43/3 (1993): 385-402.

0061 Course, John E. *Speech and Response: A Rhetorical Analysis of the Introductions to the Speeches of the Book of Job (Chaps. 4-24)* [CBQMS, 25]. Washington (D.C.): Catholic Biblical Association, 1994.

Opening Soliloquy (chap. 3)

0062 Freedman, David Noel. "The Structure of Job 3." *Bib* 49 (1968): 503-508.

0063 Cox, Dermot. "The Desire for Oblivion in Job 3." *SBFLA* 23 (1973): 37-49.

0064 Loretz, O. "Ugaritisch-Hebräisch in Job 3,3-26. Zum Disput von M. Dahood und J. Barr." *UF* 8 (1976): 123-127.

0065 Morre, R.D. "The Integrity of Job." *CBQ* 45 (1983): 17-31.

0066 Perdue, Leo G. "Job's Assault on Creation." *HAR* 10 (1986): 295-315.

0067 Cox, C. "The Wrath of God Has Come to Me: Job's First Speech according to the Septuagint." *SR* 16 (1987): 195-204.

0068 Blumenthal, Elke. "Hiob und die Harfnerlieder." *TLZ* 115 (1990): 721-730.

0069 Chiolerio, Marco. "Giobbe invoca la morte: paura o desiderio?" *Teresianum* 43 (1992): 27-52.

0070 Jacobsen, Thorkild and Kirsten Nielsen. "Cursing the Day." *SJT* 6 (1992): 187-204.

0071 Beuken, W.A.M. "Job's Imprecation as the Cradle of a New Religious Discourse. The Perplexing Impact of the Semantic Correspondence between Job 3, Job 4-5 and Job 6-7." In W. Beuken (ed.). *The Book of Job* [BETL, 114]. Leuven: University Press, 1994, pp. 41-78.

0072 Bezuidenhout, L.C. "Semantiese ritme en beweging in Job 3: 'n ander benandering tot die waardering van die teks." *HerTS* 50 (1994): 236-245.

0073 Perdue, L.G. "Metaphorical Theology in the Book of Job: Theological Anthropology in the First Cycle of Job's Speeches (Job 3; 6-7; 9-10)." In W. Beuken (ed.). *The Book of Job* [BETL, 114]. Leuven: University Press, 1994, pp. 129-156.

0074 O'Connor, Kathleen M. "Job Uncreates the World." *TBT* 34/1 (1996): 4-8.

3:3-13

    0075   Fishbane, M. "Jeremiah iv 23-26 and Job iii 3-13: A Recovered Use of the Creation Pattern." *VT* 21 (1971): 151-167.

3:3

    0076   Blank, S.H. "'Perish the Day!' A Misdirected Curse (Job 3:3)." *BIES* 19 (1955): 65-69.

3:6

    0077   Rendsburg, G. "Double Polysemy in Genesis 49:6 and Job 3:6." *CBQ* 44 (1982): 48-51.

3:8

    0078   Ullendorff, E. "Job iii 8." *VT* 11 (1961): 350-351.

    0078a   van Duin, Kees. "Der Gegner Israels: Leviatan in Hiob 3:8." In Janet Dyk (ed.). *Give Ear to My Words: Psalms and Other Poetry in and around the Hebrew Bible* [festschrift for N.A. van Uchelen]. Kampen: Kok Pharos, 1996, pp. 153-159.

3:25

    0079   Katz, Robert L. "A Psychoanalytic Comment on Job 3:25." *HUCA* 29 (1958): 377-383.

First Cycle of Speeches (chaps. 4-14)

    0080   Michel, Walter L. *Job in the Light of Northwest Semitic*, vol I: Prologue and First Cycle of Speeches (Job 1:1 — 14:22) [BibOr, 42]. Rome: Pontifical Biblical Institute, 1987.

    0081   Waddle, Sharon H. "Dubious Praise: The Form and Context of the Participial Hymns in Job 4-14." Dissertation, Vanderbilt, 1987.

    0082   van der Lugt, Pieter. "Stanza-Structure and Word-Repetition in Job 3-14." *JSOT* 40 (1988): 3-38.

0083 van Rensburg, J.F.J. "Wise Men Saying Things by Asking Questions: The Function of the Interrogative in Job 3-14." *OTE* 4/2 (1991): 227-247.

Eliphaz (4-5)

0084 Gillischewski, E. "Die erste Elifaz-Rede Hiob Kap. 4 und 5." *ZAW* 39 (1921): 290-296.

0085 Fullerton, K. "Double Entendre in the First Speech of Eliphaz." *JBL* 49 (1930): 320-374.

0086 Asensio, F. "La visión de Elifaz y su proyección sapiencial." *EstBib* 35 (1976): 145-163.

0087 Berg, W. "Gott und der Gerechte in der Rahmenerzählung des Buches Hiob." *MTZ* 31 (1981): 206-221.

0088 Miller, James E. "The Vision of Eliphaz as Foreshadowing in the Book of Job." *PEGLMBS* 9 (1989): 98-112.

0089 Cotter, David. *A Study of Job 4-5 in the Light of Contemporary Literary Theory* [SBLDS, 124]. Atlanta: Scholars, 1992.

0090 Chbeir, T. "Justice rétributive et construction de la réalité dans le premier discours d'Éliphaz (Jb 4-5): analyse et évaluation." Dissertation, Pontifical Gregorian University (Rome), 1993.

0091 Beuken, W.A.M. "Job's Imprecation as the Cradle of a New Religious Discourse. The Perplexing Impact of the Semantic Correspondence between Job 3, Job 4-5 and Job 6-7." In W. Beuken (ed.). *The Book of Job* [BETL, 114]. Leuven: University Press, 1994, pp. 41-78.

4:11

0092 Ciccarese, M.P. "Il formicaleone, il Fisiologi e l'esegesi allegorica de Gb 4,11." *Annali di storia dell'esegesi* 11 (1994): 545-569.

4:12-21

    0093   Smith, Gary V. "Job iv 12-21: Is It Eliphaz's Vision?" *VT* 40 (1990): 453-463.

4:12-16

    0094   Lust, J. "A Stormy Vision: Some Remarks on Job 4,12-16." *Bijdr* 36 (1975): 308-311.

4:13

    0095   Clines, David J.A. "Job 4,13: A Byronic Suggestion." *ZAW* 92 (1980): 289-291.

4:15

    0096   Dahood, Mitchell. "'Storm' in Job 4,15." *Bib* 48 (1967): 544-545.

    0097   Paul, Shalom M. "Job 4,15 - a Hair-Raising Encounter." *ZAW* 95 (1983): 119-121.

4:19

    0098   Rimbach, James A. "'Crushed before the moth' (Job 4:19)." *JBL* 100 (1981): 244-246.

4:20-21

    0099   Clines, David J.A. "Verb Modality and the Interpretation of Job iv 20-21." *VT* 30 (1980): 354-357.

5:1-8

    0100   Clines, D.J.A. "Job 5, 1-8: A New Exegesis." *Bib* 62 (1981): 185-194.

5:3

    0101   Brin, Gershon. "Job v 3 — Textual Text Case: The Translator's Limits of Consideration." *VT* 42 (1992): 391-393.

5:5

    0102 Wolfers, David. "A Note on Job v 3." *VT* 43 (1993): 274-276.

5:7

    0103 Driver, G.R. "On Job v 5." *TZ* 12 (1956): 485-486.

5:9-16

    0104 Wolfers, David. "Sparks Flying? Job 5:7." *JBQ* 23 (1995): 3-8.

5:17-23

    0105 Crenshaw, James L. "The Influence of the Wise upon Amos: The 'Doxologies of Amos' and Job 5,9-16; 9,5-10." *ZAW* 79 (1967): 42-52.

5:21

    0106 Burns, John Barclay. "The Chastening of the Just in Job 5:17-23: Four Strikes of Erra." *PEGLMBS* 10 (1990): 18-30.

5:23

    0107 Burns, John Barclay. "The *šwt lšwn* in Job 5:21a as Metaphor and Irony." *BZ* 35 (1991): 93-96.

    0108 Beer, G. "Zu Hiob 5:23." *ZAW* 35 (1915): 63-64.

Job (6-7)

    0109 Cox, Claude. "The Wrath of God Has Come to Me: Job's First Speech according to the Septuagint." *SR* 16 (1987): 195-204.

    0110 Beuken, W.A.M. "Job's Imprecation as the Cradle of a New Religious Discourse. The Perplexing Impact of the Semantic Correspondence between Job 3, Job 4-5 and Job 6-7." In W. Beuken (ed.). *The Book of Job* [BETL, 114]. Leuven: University Press, 1994, pp. 41-78.

0111 Perdue, L.G. "Metaphorical Theology in the Book of Job: Theological Anthropology in the First Cycle of Job's Speeches (Job 3; 6-7; 9-10)." In W. Beuken (ed.). *The Book of Job* [BETL, 114]. Leuven: University Press, 1994, pp. 129-156.

6:2-3

0112 Sutcliffe, E.F. "Further Notes on Job, Textual and Exegetical: 6,2-3,13; 8,16-17; 19,20.26." *Bib* 31 (1950): 365-378.

6:4

0113 Fontaine, Carole R. "'Arrows of the Almighty' (Job 6:4): Perspectives on Pain." *ATR* 66 (1984): 243-251.

6:6

0114 Millard, A.R. "What Has No Taste? (Job 6,6)." *UF* 1 (1969): 210.

6:8-10

0115 Riggans, Walter. "A Note on Job 6:8-10: Suicide and Death Wishes." *Dor le Dor* 15 (1986-87): 173-176.

0116 Riggans, Walter. "Job 6:8-10: Short Comments." *ExpTim* 99 (1987): 45-46.

6:10

0117 Mers, M. "A Note on Job vi 10." *VT* 32 (1982): 234-236.

6:13

0118 Sutcliffe, E.F. "Further Notes on Job, Textual and Exegetical: 6,2-3,13; 8,16-17; 19,20.26." *Bib* 31 (1950): 365-378.

6:16

0119 Skehan, Patrick W. "Second Thoughts on Job 6:16 and 6:25." *CBQ* 31 (1969): 210-212.

6:18

0120 Sutcliffe, E.F. "Notes on Job, Textual and Exegetical: 6,18; 11,12; 31,35; 34,17.20; 36,27-33; 37,1." *Bib* 30 (1949): 66-90.

6:25

0121 Doniach, W.S. and W.E. Barnes. "Job vi 25." *JTS* 31 (1929-30): 291-292.

0122 Skehan, Patrick W. "Second Thoughts on Job 6:16 and 6:25." *CBQ* 31 (1969): 210-212.

7:6-7

0122a Noegel, Scott B. "Janus Parallelism in Job and Its Literary Significance." *JBL* 115 (1996): 313-320.

7:6

0123 Szpek, Heidi M. "The Peshitta on Job 7:6 - 'My days are swifter(?) than an *'RG'*." *JBL* 113 (1994): 287-290.

7:8

0124 Gorea, M. "Job 7,8: une contribution à la problématique des versets portant astérisque dans la Septante." In W. Beuken (ed.). *The Book of Job* [BETL, 114]. Leuven: University Press, 1994, pp. 430-434.

7:10

0125 Jacob, B. "Erklärung einiger Hiob-Stellen: 7:10, 7:16." *ZAW* 32 (1912): 282-283.

7:12

0126 Dahood, Mitchell. "'Muzzle,' in Job 7:12." *JBL* 80 (1961): 70-71.

0127 Diewert, David A. "Job 7:12: *Yam, Tannin* and the Surveillance of Job." *JBL* 106 (1987): 203-215.

0128 Janzen, J. Gerald. "Another Look at God's Watch Over Job (7:12)." *JBL* 108 (1989): 109-113.

7:16

0129 Jacob, B. "Erklärung einiger Hiob-Stellen: 7:10, 7:16." *ZAW* 32 (1912): 282-283.

7:23-24

0129a Noegel, Scott B. "Janus Parallelism in Job and Its Literary Significance." *JBL* 115 (1996): 313-320.

Bildad (8)

0130 Löhr, M. "Die drei Bildad-Reden im Buche Hiob." In K. Marti (ed.). *Beiträge zur alttestamentliche Wissenschaft* [festschrift for K. Budde; BZAW, 34]. Berlin: A. Töpelmann, 1920, pp. 107-112.

0131 Irwin, W.A. "The First Speech of Bildad." *ZAW* 51 (1953): 205-216.

8:16-17

0132 Sutcliffe, E.F. "Further Notes on Job, Textual and Exegetical: 6,2-3,13; 8,16-17; 19,20.26." *Bib* 31 (1950): 365-378.

Job (9-10)

0133 Fullerton, K. "On Job 9 and 10." *JBL* 53 (1934): 321-349.

0134 Fullerton, K. "Job, Chapters 9 and 10." *AJSL* 55 (1938): 225-269.

0135 Roberts, J.J.M. "Job's Summons to Yahweh: The Exploitation of a Legal Metaphor." *ResQ* 16 (1973): 159-165.

0136 Perdue, L.G. "Metaphorical Theology in the Book of Job: Theological Anthropology in the First Cycle of Job's Speeches (Job 3; 6-7; 9-10)." In W. Beuken (ed.). *The Book of Job* [BETL, 114]. Leuven: University Press, 1994, pp. 129-156.

9:5-10

0137 Crenshaw, James L. "The Influence of the Wise upon Amos: The 'Doxologies of Amos' and Job 5,9-16; 9,5-10." *ZAW* 79 (1967): 42-52.

9:9

0138 Herz, N. "The Astral Terms in Job IX 9, XXXVIII 31-32." *JTS* 14 (1913): 575-577.

0139 Hess, J.-J. "Die Sternbilder in Hiob 9,9 und 38,31f." In T. Menzel (ed.) *Festschrift Georg Jacob*. Leipzig: Harrassowitz, 1932, pp. 94-99.

9:12

0140 Xella, P. "*HTP* 'uccidere, annientare' in *Giobbe* 9,12." *Henoch* 1 (1979): 337-341.

9:21

0141 Paul, S.M. "An Unrecognized Medical Idiom in Canticles 6,12 and Job 9,21." *Bib* 59 (1978): 545-547.

9:23

0142 Zimmermann, F. "Note on Job 9:23." *JTS* ns 2 (1951): 164-165.

9:25

0143 Zurro, E. "Disemia de *brh* y paralelismo birfonte en Job 9,25." *Bib* 62 (1981): 546-547.

9:31

0144 Pope, Marvin H. "The Word *šahat* in Job 9:31." *JBL* 83 (1964): 269-278.

9:32-33

    0145 Sacchi, Paolo. "Giobbe e il patto (Giobbe 9, 32-33)." *Henoch* 4 (1982): 175-183.

9:35

    0146 Joüon, P. "Notes philologiques sure le texte hébreu de Job 1,5; 9,35; 12,21; 28,1; 28,27; 29,14." *Bib* 11 (1930): 322-324.

10:8

    0147 Reider, J. "Some Notes to the Text of the Scriptures, 10 - Job 10,8." *HUCA* 3 (1926): 113.

10:15

    0148 Jacob, B. "Erklärung einiger Hiob-Stellen, 10:15." *ZAW* 32 (1912): 278-287.

10:16

    0149 Stec, D.M. "The Targum Rendering of *WYG'H* in Job x 16." *VT* 34 (1984): 367-368.

10:17

    0150 Watson, Wilfred. "The Metaphor in Job 10,17." *Bib* 63 (1982): 255-257.

Zophar (11)

    0151 de Regt, L.J. "Implications of Rhetorical Questions in Strophes in Job 11 and 15." In W. Beuken (ed.). *The Book of Job* [BETL, 114]. Leuven: University Press, 1994, pp. 321-328.

11:6

    0152 Slotki, J.J. "Job xi 6." *VT* 35 (1985): 229-230.

11:11

0153 Jacob, B. "Erklärung einiger Hiob-Stellen, 11:11." *ZAW* 32 (1912): 278-287.

11:12

0154 Sutcliffe, E.F. "Notes on Job, Textual and Exegetical: 6,18; 11,12; 31,35; 34,17.20; 36,27-33; 37,1." *Bib* 30 (1949): 66-90.

Job (12-14)

0155 Wolfers, David. "Greek Logic in the Book of Job (chapter 12)." *Dor le Dor* 15 (1986-87): 166-172.

0156 Swanepoel, M.G. "Job 12 — An(other) Anticipation of the Voice from the Whirlwind?" *OTE* 4 (1991): 192-205.

0157 Chin, Catherine. "Job and the Injustice of God: Implicit Arguments in Job 13.17 - 14.12." *JSOT* 64 (1994): 91-101.

0158 Wolfers, David. "Reflections on Job xii." *VT* 44 (1994): 401-406.

12:2

0159 Davies, J.A. "A Note on Job xii 2." *VT* 25 (1975): 670-671.

12:6

0160 Jacob, B. "Erklärung einiger Hiob-Stellen: 12:6; 14:11; 14:16; 14:22." *ZAW* 32 (1912): 278-287.

12:7-9

0161 De Gugliemo, A. "Job 12:7-9 and the Knowability of God." *CBQ* 6 (1944): 476-482.

12:19

0162 Sarna, N.M. "Job 12:19." *JBL* 74 (1955): 272-273.

12:21

0163 Joüon, P. "Notes philologiques sure le texte hébreu de Job 1,5; 9,35; 12,21; 28,1; 28,27; 29,14." *Bib* 11 (1930): 322-324.

13:7-14:12

0164 Chin, C. "Job and the Injustice of God: Implicit Arguments in Job 13,17 - 14,12." *JSOT* 64 (1994) 91-101.

14:4-5

0165 Manni, Marialuisa Annecchino. "Iob 14,4-5 nella lettura dei Padri." *Aug* 32 (1992): 237-259.

14:4

0166 Zink, J.K. "Uncleanness and Sin in Job xiv 4 and Ps li 7." *VT* 17 (1967): 354-361.

14:12

0167 Orlinsky, H.M. "The Hebrew and Greek Texts of Job 14.12." *JQR* 28 (1937-38): 57-68.

14:20

0168 Haplern, B. "Yhwh's Summary Justice in Job xiv 20." *VT* 28 (1978): 472-474.

Second Cycle of Speeches (chaps. 15-21)

0169 Samudi, Joseph. "A Study of the Second Cycle of Speeches in the Book of Job." *Beth Mikra* 112 (1987): 63-68.

Eliphaz (15)

0170 Hoffmann, G. "Ergänzungen und Berichtigungen zu Hiob." *ZAW* 49 (1931): 141-145.

0171 de Regt, L.J. "Implications of Rhetorical Questions in Stophes in Job 11 and 15." In W. Beuken (ed.). *The Book of Job* [BETL, 114]. Leuven: University Press, 1994, pp. 321-328.

15:4-5

0172 Wolfers, D. "Job 15,4.5: An Exploration." In W. Beuken (ed.). *The Book of Job* [BETL, 114]. Leuven: University Press, 1994, pp. 382-386.

Job (16-17)

0173 Curtis, John B. "On Job's Witness in Heaven." *JBL* 102 (1983): 549-562.

16:4

0174 Loretz, O. "*HBR* in Job 16:4." *CBQ* 23 (1961): 293-294.

16:20

0175 Vella, P. "Il redentore di Giobbe [16,20]." *RivB* 13 (1965): 161-168.

0176 Gross, Carl D. "Notes on the Meaning of Job xvi 20." *VT* 42 (1992): 391-393.

17:6

0177 Jacob, B. "Erklärung einiger Hiob-Stellen: 17,6." *ZAW* 32 (1912): 278-287.

Bildad (18)

0178 Löhr, M. "Die drei Bildad-Reden im Buche Hiob." In K. Marti (ed.). *Beiträge zur alttestamentliche Wissenschaft* [festschrift for K. Budde; BZAW, 34]. Berlin: A. Töpelmann, 1920, pp. 107-112.

0179 Sarna, N.M. "The Mythological Background of Job 18." *JBL* 82 (1963): 315-318.

18:2-3

0180 Wolfers, David. "Three Singular Plurals, Job 18:2,3." *JBQ* 22/1 (1994): 21-25.

18:5-21

0181 Burns, John Barclay. "The Mythological Background to Job 18, 5-21." *BeO* 33 (1991): 129-140.

18:13

0182 Burns, John Barclay. "The Identity of Death's First-Born (Job xviii 13)." *VT* 37 (1987): 362-364.

0183 Wyatt, Nicolas. "The Expression *bekôr māwet* in Job 18:13 and Its Mythological Background." *VT* 40 (1990): 207-216.

0184 Burns, John Barclay. "*Nartaru* and *Nergal* — Down But Not Out: A Reply to Nicolas Wyatt." *VT* 43 (1993): 1-9.

Job (19)

0185 Mowinckel, S. "Hiobs *gō'ēl* und Zeuge im Himmel." *BZAW* 41 (1925): 207-212.

0186 Garcia Cordero, M. "La tesis de la sanción moral y la esperanza de la recurrección en el libro de Job." In *La encíclica Humani Generis* [XII Semaña Bíblica Española]. Madrid: Libreria Cientifica Medinaceli, 1952, pp. 571-594.

0187 Garcia Cordero, M. "La esperanza de la recurrección corporal en Job." *Ciencia Tomista* 80 (1953): 1-23.

0188 Galling, K. "Die Grabinschrift Hiobs." *WO* 2 (1954-59): 303-307.

0189 Irwin, W.A. "Job's Redeemer." *JBL* 81 (1962): 217-229.

0190 Blumenthal, D.R. "A Play on Words in the Nineteenth Chapter of Job." *VT* 16 (1966): 497-501.

0191 Wolfers, David. "Jot, Tittle and *Waw*." *DD* 17 (1988-89): 230-236.

0192 Althann, R. "Job and the Idea of the Beatific Afterlife." *OTE* 4 (1991): 316-326.

19:14-15

0193 Kutsch, Ernst. "Text und Textgeschichte in Hiob XIX: zu Problemen in v. 14-15, 20, 23-24." *VT* 32 (1982): 464-484.

19:15

0194 Ratner, Robert. "The 'Feminine Takes Precedence' Syntagm and Job 19,15." *ZAW* 102 (1990): 238-251.

19:19

0195 Penar, T. "Job 19,19 in the Light of Ben Sirach 6,11." *Bib* 48 (1967): 293-295.

19:20

0196 Sutcliffe, E.F. "Further Notes on Job, Textual and Exegetical: 6,2-3,13; 8,16-17; 19,20.26." *Bib* 31 (1950): 365-378.

0197 Kutsch, Ernst. "Text und Textgeschichte in Hiob XIX: zu Problemen in v. 14-15, 20, 23-24." *VT* 32 (1982): 464-484.

19:21-29

0198 Christo, Gordon E. "The Eschatological Judgment in Job 19: 21-29 — an Exegetical Study." Dissertation, Andrews, 1992.

19:23-29

0199 Zuck, Roy B. "The Certainty of Seeing God: A Brief Exposition of Job 19:23-29." In *Sitting with Job: Selected Studies on the Book of Job*. Grand Rapids: Baker, 1992, pp. 279-281.

19:23-27

    0200 Waterman, L. "Note on Job 19:23-27: Job's Triumph of Faith." *JBL* 69 (1950): 379-380.

    0201 Clines, David. "Belief, Desire and Wish in Job 19:23-27 — Clues for the Identity of Job's 'Redeemer'." In M. Augustin and K.-D. Schunk (eds.). *"Wünschet Jerusalem Frieden": Collected Communications to the XIIth Congress of the International Organization for the Study of the Old Testament, Jerusalem 1986.* [BEATAJ, 13]. Frankfurt: Lang, 1988, pp. 363-370.

19:23-24

    0202 Kutsch, Ernst. "Text und Textgeschichte in Hiob XIX: zu Problemen in v. 14-15, 20, 23-24." *VT* 32 (1982): 464-484.

19:23

    0203 Ebach, J. "Die 'Schrift' in Hiob 19,23." In Rüdiger Liwak and Siegfried Wagner (eds.). *Prophetie und geschichtliche Wirklichkeit im alten Israel* [festschrift for Siegfried Hermann]. Stuttgart: Kohlhammer, 1991, pp. 99-121.

19:24

    0204 Stamm, J.J. "Versuch zur Erklärung von Hiob 19,24." *TZ* 4 (1948): 331-338.

    0205 Stamm, J.J. "Zu Hiob 19,24." *ZAW* 65 (1953): 302.

    0206 Baker, A. "The Strange Case of Job's Chisel (19:24)." *CBQ* 31 (1969): 370-379.

19:25-29

    0207 Bruston, C. "Pour l'exégèse de Job 19,25-29." *ZAW* 26 (1906): 143-146.

19:25-27

0208 Speer, J. "Zur Exegese von Hiob 19,25-27." *ZAW* 25 (1905): 47-140.

0209 Hudal, A. "Textkritische und exegetische Bemerkungen zu Ijob 19:25-27." *BZ* (1916-17): 214-235.

0210 Hölscher, G. "Hiob 19,25-27 und Jubil 23,30-31." *ZAW* 12 (1935): 277-283.

0211 Zink, J.K. "Impatient Job: An Interpretation of Job 19:25-27." *JBL* 84 (1965): 147-152.

0212 Prado, J. "La perspectiva escatológica en Job 19,25-27." *EstBib* 25 (1966): 143-153.

0213 Michel, Walter L. "Confidence and Despair: Job 19,25-27 in the Light of Northwest Semitic Studies." In W. Beuken (ed.). *The Book of Job* [BETL, 114]. Leuven: University Press, 1994, pp. 157-182.

19:25

0214 Beauchamp, É. "Le goël de Job 19,25." *LTP* 33 (1977): 309.

0215 Barré, M.L. "A Note on Job xix 25." *VT* 29 (1979): 107-110.

0216 Mende, Theresia. " 'Ich weiss, dass mein Erloser lebt' (Ijob 19:25)." *TTZ* 99 (1990): 15-35.

0217 Kessler, Rainer. "'Ich weiss, dass mein Erlöser lebt.' Sozialgeschichtlicher Hintergrund und theologische Bedeutung der Löser-Vorstellung in Hiob 19,25." *ZTK* 89 (1992): 139-158.

0218 Holman, J. "Does My Redeemer Live or Is My Redeemer the Living God? Some Reflections on the Translation of Job 19,25." In W. Beuken (ed.). *The Book of Job* [BETL, 114]. Leuven: University Press, 1994, pp. 377-381.

19:26

    0219   Sutcliffe, E.F. "Further Notes on Job, Textual and Exegetical: 6,2-3,13; 8,16-17; 19,20.26." *Bib* 31 (1950): 365-378.

    0220   Gaster, T.H. "Short Notes: Job xix 26." *VT* 4 (1954): 73-79.

19:29

    0221   Fisher, L.R. "*šdyn* in Job xix 29." *VT* 11 (1961): 342-343.

Zophar (20)

    0222   Kelly, B.H. "Truth in Contradiction: A Study of Job 20 and 21." *Int* 15 (1961): 147-156.

    0223   Holbert, J.C. "'The skies will uncover his iniquity': Satire in the Second Speech of Zophar (Job 20)." *VT* 31 (1981): 171-179.

20:14

    0224   Pardee, D. "'Venom' in Job 20,14." *ZAW* 91 (1979): 401-416.

Job (21)

    0225   Kelly, B.H. "Truth in Contradiction: A Study of Job 20 and 21." *Int* 15 (1961): 147-156.

    0226   Willi-Plein, I. "Hiobs immer aktuelle Frage." *Meddelander från Stiftelsens för Åbo* 47 (1979): 122-136.

    0227   Talstra, E. "Dialogue in Job 21: 'Virtual quotations' or Text Grammatical Markers?" In W. Beuken (ed.). *The Book of Job* [BETL, 114]. Leuven: University Press, 1994, pp. 329-348.

21:23-26

    0228   Knauf, E.A. "Zum Text von Hi 21, 23-26." *BN* 7 (1978): 22-24.

Third Cycle of Speeches (chaps. 22-27)

0229 Martin, G.W. "Elihu and the Third Cycle in the Book of Job." Dissertation, Princeton, 1972.

0230 Wolfers, David. "Job: The Third Cycle." *Dor le Dor* 17/1 (1988): 19-25.

0231 Redditt, Paul L. "Reading the Speech Cycles in the Book of Job." *HAR* 14 (1994): 205-214.

0232 Wahl, Harald Martin. "Elihu, Frevler oder Frommer? Die Audlegung des Hiobbuches (HI 32-37) durch ein Pesudepigraphon (TestHi 41-43)." *JSJ* 25 (June 1994): 1-17.

0233 Witte, Markkus. *Vom Leiden zur Lehre: Der dritte Redegang (Hiob 21-27) und die Redakstionsgeschichte des Hiobbuches* [BZAW, 230]. Berlin: de Gruyter, 1994.

0234 Witte, Markus. *Philologische Notizen zu Hiob 21-27* [BZAW, 234]. Berlin: de Gruyter, 1995.

Eliphaz (22)

22:29-30

0235 Gordis, Robert. "Corporate Personality in Job: A Note on 22:29-30." *JNES* 4 (1945): 54.

22:30

0236 Thexton, Clive. "Contributions and Comments: A Note on Job 22:30." *ExpTim* 78/11 (1967): 342, 343.

Job (23-24)

23:2

0237 de Wilde, A. "Eine alte Crux Interpretum, Hiob xxiii 2." *VT* 22 (1972): 368-374.

24:1-25

    0238   Loretz, O. "Philologische und textologische Probleme in Hi 24,1-25." *UF* 12 (1980): 261-266.

24:19-20

    0239   Burns, John Barclay. "Support for the Emendation *rĕhōb mĕgōmô* in Job xxiv 19-20." *VT* 39 (1989): 480-485.

    0240   Geyer, J.B. "Mythological Sequence in Job xxiv 19-20." *VT* 42 (1992): 118-120.

*** (25-27)

    0241   Reventlow, Henning. "Tradition und Redaktion in Hiob 27 im Rahmen der Hiobreden des Abschnittes Hi 24-27." *ZAW* 94 (1982): 279-292.

    0242   Wolfers, David. "Job: The Third Cycle." *DD* 17/1 (1988): 19-25.

    0243   Wolfers, David. "The Speech-Cycles in the Book of Job." *VT* 43/3 (1993): 385-402.

ch. 25

    0244   Witte, M. "Die dritte Rede Bildads (Hiob 25) und die Redaktionsgeschichte des Hiobbuches." In W. Beuken (ed.). *The Book of Job* [BETL, 114]. Leuven: University Press, 1994, pp. 349-355.

ch. 26

    0245   Wolfers, D. "Job 26: An Orphan Chapter." In W. Beuken (ed.). *The Book of Job* [BETL, 114]. Leuven: University Press, 1994, pp. 387-391.

    0245a   Hermisson, Hans-Jürgen. "Ein Bibeltext für Fortgeschrittene (Hiob 26)." *Theologische Beiträge* 96 (1996): 137-144.

26:5-14

    0246 Gross, Heinrich. "Die Allmacht des Schöpfergottes: Erwägungen zu Hiob 26,5-14." In Josef Zmijewski (ed.). *Die alttestamentliche Botschaft als Wegweisung* [festschrift for Heinz Reinelt]. Stuttgart: Katholisches Bibelwerk, 1990, pp. 75-84.

26:7

    0247 Roberts, J.J.M. "*sāpōn* in Job 26,7." *Bib* 56 (1975): 554-557.

Poem on Wisdom (chap. 28)

    0248 von Rad, Gerhard. "Hiob xxviii und die altägyptische Weisheit." In M. Noth and D. Winton-Thomas (eds.). *Wisdom in Israel and in the Ancient Near East* [festschrift for H.H. Rowley; VTSup, 3]. Leiden: Brill, 1955, pp. 293-301.

    0249 Settlemire, C.C. "The Meaning, Importance and Original Position of Job 28." Dissertation, Drew University, 1969.

    0250 Niccacci, Alviero. "Giobbe 28." *SBFLA* 31 (1981): 29-58.

    0251 Clark, David J. "In Search of Wisdom: Notes on Job 28." *BT* 33 (1982): 401-405.

    0252 Geller, Stephen A. "Where Is Wisdom? A Literary Study of Job 28 in Its Settings." In J. Neusner (ed.). *Judaic Perspectives on Ancient Israel*. Philadelphia: Fortress, 1987, pp. 155-188.

    0253 van der Lugt, Pieter. "The Form and Function of the Refrains in Job 28: Some Comments Relating to the Strophic Structure of Hebrew Poetry." In W. van der Meer (ed.). *The Structural Analysis of Biblical and Canaanite Poetry* [JSOTSup, 74]. Sheffield 1988, pp. 265-293.

    0254 Wolfers, David. "The Volcano in Job 28." *JBQ* 18 (1989-90): 234-240.

    0255 Cook, Johann. "Aspects of Wisdom in the Texts of Job (Chapter 28) — *Vorlage(n)* and/or Translator(s)?" *OTE* 5 (1992): 26-45.

0256　Hill, Robert C. "Job in Search of Wisdom." *ScrB* 23 (1993): 34-38.

0257　van Oorschot, J. "Hiob 28: Die verborgene Weisheit und die Furcht Gottes als Überwindung einer generalisierten חכמה." In W. Beuken (ed.). *The Book of Job* [BETL, 114]. Leuven: University Press, 1994, pp. 183-202.

0258　Wolfers, David. "The Stone of Deepest Darkness: A Mineralogical Mystery (Job xxviii)." *VT* 44 (1994): 274-276.

0259　Zimmermann, R. "Homo Sapiens Ignorans: Hiob 28 als Bestandteil der ursprünglichen Hiobdichtung." *BN* 74 (1994): 80-100.

0260　Mulrooney, Joe. "Where Shall Wisdom Be Found, and Where Is the Place of Misunderstanding?" *Month* 28 (1995): 341-344.

0261　Petersen, Mike. "Job 28: The Theological Center of the Book of Job." *BVC* 29/1 (1995): 99-111.

28:1

0262　Joüon, P. "Notes philologiques sure le texte hébreu de Job 1,5; 9,35; 12,21; 28,1; 28,27; 29,14." *Bib* 11 (1930): 322-324.

28:4

0263　Dick, Michael B. "Job xxviii 4: A New Translation." *VT* 29 (1979): 216-221.

28:27

0264　Harris, Scott. "Wisdom or Creation? A New Interpretation of Job xxviii 27." *VT* 33 (1983): 419-427.

Closing Soliloquy (chaps. 29-31)

0265　Skehan, P.W. "Job's Final Plea (Job 29-31) and the Lord's Reply (Job 38-41)." *Bib* 45 (1964): 51-61.

0266 Kautz, J.R. "A Hermeneutical Study of Job 29-31." Dissertation, Southern Baptist Theological Seminary, 1970.

0267 Lévêque, Jean. "Anamnèse et disculpation: la conscience de juste en Job, 29-31." In M. Gilbert (ed.). *La Sagesse de l'Ancien Testament* [BETL, 51]. Leuven: University Press, 1979, pp. 231-248.

0268 Ceresko, Anthony R. *Job 29-31 in the Light of Northwest Semitic: A Translation and Philological Commentary* [BibOr, 36]. Roma: Pontifical Biblical Institute, 1980.

0269 Cox, Dermot. "Structure and Function of the Final Challenge: Job 29-31." *PIBA* 5 (1981): 55-71.

0270 Holbert, John C. "The Rehabilitation of the Sinner: The Function of Job 29-31." *ZAW* 95 (1983): 229-237.

0271 Webster, Edwin. "Strophic Patterns in Job 29-42." *JSOT* 30 (1984): 95-109.

0272 Cox, Claude E. "Job's Concluding Soliloquy: Chs. 29-31." In *VII Congress of the International Organization for Septuagint and Cognate Studies* [SBLSBS, 31]. Atlanta: Scholars Press, 1991, pp. 325-339.

0273 Smith, William C. "The Function of Chapters 29-31 in the Book of Job." Dissertation, Southern Baptist Theological Seminary, 1992.

ch. 29

0274 Malchow, Bruce V. "A Royal Prototype in Job 29." In Jack C. Knight and Lawrence A. Sinclair (eds.). *The Psalms and Other Studies* [festschrift for Joseph Hunt]. Nashotah, WI: Nashotah House Seminary, 1990, pp. 178-184.

29:4

0275 Ortiz de Urtaran, Félix. "'Cuando Dios era un íntimo en mi tienda' (Job 29,4)." *Lumen* 33 (1984): 289-309.

29:14

0276 Joüon, P. "Notes philologiques sure le texte hébreu de Job 1,5; 9,35; 12,21; 28,1; 28,27; 29,14." *Bib* 11 (1930): 322-324.

29:18

0277 Dahood, Mitchell. "*hôl* 'phoenix' in Job 29:18 and in Ugaritic." *CBQ* 36 (1974): 85-88.

30:2-8

0278 Yamaga, Tetsuo. "'Can the roots of the broom be eaten?' - A Proposal for the Interpretation of Job 30:2-8." *Annual of the Japanese Biblical Institute* 10 (1984): 20-32.

0279 Ceresko, Anthony R. "The Option for the Poor in the Book of Job [on 30:2-8]." *ITS* 26 (1989): 105-121.

30:4

0280 Kuhm, Hanni. "Why are Job's Opponents Still Made to Eat Broom-Root? (30:4)." *BT* 40 (1989): 332-336.

30:18

0281 Wolfers, David. "The 'neck' of Job's tunic (Job xxx 18)." *VT* 44 (1994): 570-572.

31

0282 Blank, S.H. "An Effective Literary Device in Job 31." *JJS* 2 (1951): 105-107.

0283 Tang, S.Y. "The Ethical Context of Job 31: A Comparative Study." Dissertation, Edinburgh, 1966-67.

0284 Osswald, E. "Hiob 31 im Rahmen der alttestamentliche Ethik." In J. Rogge (ed.). *Theologische Versuche*. Berlin 1970, pp. 9-26.

0285 Fohrer, Georg. "The Righteous Man in Job 31." In *Essays in Old Testament Ethics* [festschrift for J. Philip Hyatt]. New York 1974, pp. 1-22.

0286 Dick, M.B. "Job 31: A Form-Critical Study." Dissertation, Johns Hopkins University, 1977.

0287 Dick, Michael Brennan. "The Legal Metaphor in Job 31." *CBQ* 41 (1979): 37-50.

0288 Dick, Michael B. "Job 31, the Oath of Innocence, and the Sage." *ZAW* 95 (1983): 31-53.

0289 Oeming, Manfred. "Ethik in der Spätzeit des Alten Testaments am Beispiel von Hiob 31 und Tobit 4." In Peter Mommer and Winfried Thiel (eds.). *Altes Testament Forschung und Wirkung* [festschrift for Hennung Graf Reventlow]. Frankfurt am Main: Peter Lang, 1994, pp. 159-173.

0290 Oeming, M. "Hiob 31 und der Dekalog." In W. Beuken (ed.). *The Book of Job* [BETL, 114]. Leuven: University Press, 1994, pp. 362-368.

31:1

0291 Michel, Walter L. "*Btwlh* 'virgin' or 'Virgin (Anath)' in Job 31:1." *Hebrew Studies* 23 (1982): 59-66.

31:35

0292 Sutcliffe, E.F. "Notes on Job, Textual and Exegetical: 6,18; 11,12; 31,35; 34,17.20; 36,27-33; 37,1." *Bib* 30 (1949): 66-90.

31:38-40

0293 van Selms, A. "Job 31:38-40 in Ugaritic Light." *Semitics* 8 (1982): 30-42.

Speeches of Elihu (chaps. 32-37)

0294 Fohrer, Georg. "Die Weisheit des Elihu." *Archive für Orientforschung* 19 (1959/60): 83-94.

0295 Beeby, H.D. "Elihu — Job's Mediator?" *South East Asia Journal of Theology* 7 (1965): 33-55.

0296 Carstensen, R.N. "The Persistence of the 'Elihu' Tradition in Later Jewish Writers." *Lexington Theological Quarterly* 2/2 (1967): 37-46.

0297 Freedman, David Noel. "The Elihu Speeches in the Book of Job." *HTR* 61 (1968): 51-59.

0298 Tate, M.E. "The Speeches of Elihu." *RevExp* 68/4 (1971): 487-495.

0299 Martin, G.W. "Elihu and the Third Cycle in the Book of Job." Dissertation, Princeton, 1972.

0300 McKay, J.W. "Elihu — a Proto-Charismatic?" *ExpTim* 90 (1978): 167-171.

0301 Hemraj, S. "Elihu's 'missionary' role in Job 32-37." *Biblebhashyam* 6 (1980): 49-80.

0302 Michel, Walter L. "Job's Real Friend: Elihu." *Criterion* (Spring 1982): 29-32.

0303 Johns, Donald A. "The Literary and Theological Function of the Elihu Speeches in the Book of Job." Dissertation, St. Louis University, 1983.

0304 Habel, Norman C. "The Role of Elihu in the Design of the Book of Job." In W. Byd Barrick and John R. Spencer (eds.). *In the Shelter of Elyon*. Sheffield: JSOT, 1984.

0305 McCabe, Robert V. "The Significance of the Elihu Speeches in the Context of the Book of Job." Dissertation, Grace Theological Seminary, 1985.

0306 Wolfers, David. "Elihu: The Provenance and Content of His Speeches." *Dor le Dor* 16/2 (1987-88): 90-98.

0307 Curtis, John Briggs. "Why Were the Elihu Speeches Added to the Book of Job?" *PEGLMBS* 8 (1988): 93-100.

0308 Curtis, John Briggs. "Elihu and Deutero-Isaiah: A Study in Literary Dependence." *PEGLMBS* 10 (1990): 31-38.

0309 Mende, Theresia. *Durch Leiden zur Vollendung: die Elihureden im Buch Ijob (32-37)*. Trier: Paulinus, 1990.

0310 Diewert, David A. "The Composition of the Elihu Speeches: A Poetic and Structural Analysis." Dissertation, Toronto, 1991.

0311 Curtis, John Briggs. "Word Play in the Speeches of Elihu (Job 32-37)." *PEGLMBS* 12 (1992): 23-30.

0312 Wahl, Harald-Martin. "Seit wann gelten die Elihureden (Hi 32-37) als Einschub? Eine Bemerkung zur Forschungsgeschichte." *BN* 63 (1992): 58-61.

0313 Wahl, Harald-Martin. "Ein Beitrag zum alttestamentlichen Vergeltungsglauben am Beispiel von Hiob 32-37." *BZ* 36 (1992): 250-255.

0314 Wahl, Harald-Martin. *Der gerechte Schöpfer: eine redaktions- und theologiegeschichtliche Untersuchung der Elihureden - Hiob 32-37* [BZAW, 207]. Berlin: de Gruyter, 1993.

0315 Witte, Markus. "Noch einmal: Seit wann gelten die Elihureden in Hiobbuch (Kap. 32-37) als Einschub?" *BN* 67 (1993): 20-25.

0316 Wahl, H.-M. "Das 'Evangelium' Elihus (Hiob 32-37)." In W. Beuken (ed.). *The Book of Job* [BETL, 114]. Leuven: University Press, 1994, pp. 356-361.

0317 Wahl, H.-M. "Elihu, Frevler oder Frommer? Die Auslegung des Hiobbuches (Hi 32-37) durch ein Pseudepigraphon (TestHi 41-43). *JSJ* 25 (1994): 1-17.

0318 Viviers, H. "Die funksie van Elihu (Job 32-37) in die boek Job." *Skrif en Kerk* 16 (1995): 171-192.

ch. 32

0319 Skehan, P.W. "'I Will Speak Up' (Job 32)." *CBQ* 31 (1969): 380-382.

0320 Skehan, P.W. "The Pit (Job 33)." *CBQ* 31 (1969): 382.

33:13

0321 Dahood, Mitchell. "The Dative Suffix in Job 33,13." *Bib* 63/2 (1982): 258-259.

33:14-30

0322 Ross, J.F. "Job 33:14-30 - The Phenomenology of Lament." *JBL* 94 (1975): 38-46.

33:21

0323 Rouillard, Hedwige. "Le sens de Job 33,21." *RB* 91 (1984): 30-50.

34:17

0324 Sutcliffe, E.F. "Notes on Job, Textual and Exegetical: 6,18; 11,12; 31,35; 34,17.20; 36,27-33; 37,1." *Bib* 30 (1949): 66-90.

34:20

0325 Sutcliffe, E.F. "Notes on Job, Textual and Exegetical: 6,18; 11,12; 31,35; 34,17.20; 36,27-33; 37,1." *Bib* 30 (1949): 66-90.

34:36

0326 Dahod, Mitchell. "Ugaritic-Phoenician Forms in Job 34,36." *Bib* 62 (1981): 548-550.

0327 Wolfers, David. "Sire! (Job xxxiv 36)." *VT* 44 (1994): 566-569.

36:5

0328 Diewert, David. "Job xxxvi 5 and the Root *m's* II." *VT* 39 (1989): 71-77.

36:16

0329 Skehan, P.W. "Job 36:16." *CBQ* 16 (1954): 285-301.

36:27-30

0330 Sutcliffe, E.F. "Notes on Job, Textual and Exegetical: 6,18; 11,12; 31,35; 34,17.20; 36,27-33; 37,1." *Bib* 30 (1949): 66-90.

37:1

0331 Sutcliffe, E.F. "Notes on Job, Textual and Exegetical: 6,18; 11,12; 31,35; 34,17.20; 36,27-33; 37,1." *Bib* 30 (1949): 66-90.

37:6

0332 Curtis, John Briggs. "Some Jewish Interpretations of Job 37:6 — Midrash or Ancient Cosmogony?" *PEGLMBS* 9 (1989): 113-123.

37:19-24

0333 Niccacci, Alviero. "La conclusione di Elihu (Giobbe 37, 19-24)." In Giovanni Bottini (ed.). *Francescani in Terra Santa*. Jerusalem: Franciscan, 1982, pp. 75-82.

0334 Cowe, S. Peter. "An Armenian Job Fragment from Sinai and Its Implications." *OrChr* 76 (1992): 123-157.

THEOLOGUE (chaps. 38:1 - 42:6)

0335 Burrows, Millar. "The Voice from the Whirlwind." *JBL* 47 (1928): 117-132.

0336 Lillie, W. "The Religious Significance of the Theophany in the Book of Job." *ExpTim* 68 (1957): 355-358.

0337 MacKenzie, R.A.F. "The Purpose of the Yahweh Speeches in the Book of Job." *Bib* 40 (1959): 435-445.

0338 Fohrer, Georg. "Gottes Antwort aus dem Sturmwind." *TZ* 18 (1962): 1-24.

0339 Gordis, Robert. "The Lord Out of the Whirlwind: The Climax and Meaning of 'Job'." *Judaism* 13 (1964): 48-63.

0340   Skehan, P.W. "Job's Final Plea (Job 29-31) and the Lord's Reply (Job 38-41)." *Bib* 45 (1964): 51-61.

0341   Würthwein, Ernst. "Gott und Mensch in Dialog und Gottesreden des Buches Hiob." In *Wort und Existenz: Studien zum AT*. Göttingen: Vandenhoeck, 1970, pp. 217-295.

0342   Terrien, Samuel. "The Yahweh Speeches and Job's Responses." *RevExp* 68 (1971): 497-509.

0343   Jakubiec, C. "Objawienie Boże w Księdze Hioba." *Ruch Biblijny i Liturgiczny* 26 (1973): 248-261.

0344   Weigart, Mazal. "God's Reply to Job." *Dor le Dor* 3/1 (1974): 25-29.

0345   Preuß, Horst Dietrich. "Jahwes Antwort an Hiob und die sogennannte Hiob-literatur des alten Vorderen Orients." In H. Donner, R. Hanhart and R. Smend (eds.). *Beiträge zur alttestamentlichen Theologie* [festschrift for W. Zimmerli]. Göttingen: Vandenhoeck, 1977, pp. 323-343.

0346   Rowold, H.J. "The Theology of Creation in the Yahweh Speeches of the Book of Job as a Solution to the Problem Posed by the Book of Job." Dissertation, Concordia Seminary in Exile (Chicago), 1977.

0347   Sawicki, M. "Technological Imagery in the Yahweh Speeches. What Did Job See?" *TBT* 91 (1977): 1304-1310.

0348   Keel, Othmar. *Jahwes Entgegnung an Ijob: Eine Deutung von Ijob 38-41 vor dem Hintergrund der zeitgenössischen Bildkunst* [FRLANT, 121]. Göttingen: Vandenhoeck, 1978.

0349   Williams, James G. "Deciphering the Unspoken: The Theophany of Job." *HUCA* 49 (1978): 59-72.

0350   Bachar, S. "God's Answer to Job." *Beth Mikra* 25 (1979): 25-29.

0351   Kubina, Veronica. *Die Gottesreden im Buch Hiob: Ein Beitrag zur Diskussion um die Einheit von Hiob 38,1 - 42,6* [Freiburger theologischer studien, 115]. Freiburg: Herder, 1979.

0352 Fadeji, Samuel O. "A Critical and Interpretive Study of the Yahweh Speeches in Job 38-41." Dissertation, Southern Baptist Seminary, 1980.

0353 Ford, L.S. "The Whirlwind Addresses Job." *St. Luke's Journal of Theology* 24 (1980-81): 217-221.

0354 Lang, Bernhard. "Ein Kranker sieht seinen Gott (Hiob 38-41)." In *Wie Wird man Prophet in Israel? Aufsätze zum AT*. Düsseldorf 1980, pp. 137-148.

0355 Brenner, Athalya. "God's Answer to Job." *VT* 31 (1981): 129-137.

0356 Keel, Othmar. "Zwei kleine Beitrage zum Verstandnis der Gottesreden im Buch Ijob." *VT* 31 (1981): 220-225.

0357 François, Frère. "Une louange au-delà du désespoir. Méditation sur Job 38-42." *VSpir* 136 (1982): 47-65.

0358 Alonso Schökel, Luis. "God's Answer to Job." In C. Duquoc and C. Floristan (eds.). *Job and the Silence of God* [Concilium, 169]. Edinburgh: T&T Clark, 1983, pp. 45-51.

0359 Alter, Robert. "The Voice from the Whirlwind." *Commentary* 77 (1984): 33-41.

0360 Williams, James G. "Job's Vision: The Dialectic of Person and Presence." *HAR* 8 (1984): 259-272.

0361 O'Connor, Daniel J. "The Futility of Myth-Making in Theodicy: Job 38-41." *PIBA* 9 (1985): 81-99.

0362 Gowan, Donald E. "God's Answer to Job: How Is It an Answer?" *Horizons in Biblical Theology* 8/2 (1986): 85-102.

0363 Hubermann Scholnick, Sylvia. "Poetry in the Courtroom: Job 38-41." In E.R. Follis (ed.). *Directions in Biblical Hebrew Poetry* [JSOTSup, 40]. Sheffield: Almond Press, 1987, pp. 185-204.

0364 van Oorschot, Jürgen. *Gott als Grenze: eine literar- und redaktionsgeschichtliche Studie zu den Gottesreden des Hiobbuches* [BZAW, 170]. Berlin: de Gruyter, 1987.

0365 Han, Jin Hee. "Yahweh Replies to Job: Yahweh's Speeches in the Book of Job, a Case of Resumptive Rhetoric." Dissertation, Princeton Theological Seminary, 1988.

0366 Müller, Hans-Peter. "Gottes Antwort an Ijob und das Recht religiöser Wahrheit." *BZ* 32 (1988): 210-231.

0367 Sarrazin, Bernard. "Du rire dans la Bible? La théophanie de Job comme parodie." *RevScRel* 76 (1988): 39-56.

0368 Tsmudi, Yosef. "God's Answer to Job." *Beth Mikra* 34 (1988-89): 302-311.

0369 Tilley, Terrence. "God and the Silencing of Job." *Modern Theology* 5 (1989): 257-270.

0370 Carson, D.A. "Mystery and Faith in Job 38:1 - 42:16." In Roy B. Zuck (ed.). *Sitting with Job: Selected Studies on the Book of Job*. Grand Rapids: Baker, 1992, pp. 373-379.

0371 Vermeylen, J. "'Connais-tu les lois des cieux?' Une lecture de Job 38-41." *Le Foi et le Temps* 20 (1990): 197-210.

0372 Meiron, Menahem. "Does the Lord's Response Provide an Answer to Job's Argument?" *Beth Mikra* 37 (1991-92): 241-244.

0373 Nel, P.J. "Cosmos and Chaos: A Reappraisal of the Divine Discourses in the Book of Job." *OTE* 4 (1991): 206-226.

0374 Loader, J.A. "Seeing God with Natural Eyes: On Job and Nature." *OTE* 5/3 (1992): 346-360.

0375 Keel, Othmar. *Dieu répond à Job*. Paris: Cerf, 1993.

0376 Unsvåg, Hilde Halsteini. " 'Men nå harjeg sett deg med egne øyne.' — Et bidrag til forståelsen zv gudstalen i Jobs bok." *TTKi* 64 (1993): 21-38.

0377 Unsvåg, Hilde Halsteini. "Gudstalene in Jobs bok — monolog eller dialog." *TTKi* 65 (1994): 83-85.

0378 Kegler, Jürgen. "'Gürte wie ein Mann deine Lenden!...' Die Gottesreden im Ijob-Buch als Aufforderung zur aktiven Auseinandersetzung mit dem Leid." In H. Michael Niemann, et. al. (eds). *Nachdenken über Israel, Bible und Theologie* [festschrift for Klaus-Dietrich Schunck; BEATAJ, 37]. Frankfurt am Main: Peter Lang, 1994, pp. 217-234.

0379 Lévêque, J. "L'interprétation des discours de Yhwh (Job 38,1 - 42,6)." In W. Beuken (ed.). *The Book of Job* [BETL, 114]. Leuven: University Press, 1994, pp. 203-222.

0380 McKibben, Bill. *The Comforting Wind: God, Job and the Scale of Creation*. Grand Rapids: Eerdmans, 1994.

0381 Newsom, C.A. "The Moral Sense of Nature: Ethics in the Light of God's Speech to Job." *PSB* 15 (1994): 9-27.

0382 Lundberg, Marilyn J. "'So that hidden things may be brought to light' - A Concept Analysis of the Yahweh-speeches in the Book of Job." Dissertation, Claremont Graduate School, 1995.

0383 Ruíz, Jean-Pierre. "Contexts in Conversation: First World and Third World Readings of Job." *Journal of Hispanic/Latino Theology* 2 (Fall 1995): 5-29.

0383a Brüning, Christian. "Kleine Schule des Staunens: Die Gottesreden im Ijobbuch." *Erbe und Auftrag* 72 (1996): 385-413.

0383b Greenstein, Edward L. "A Forensic Understanding of the Speech from the Whirlwind." In Michael Fox, et al (eds.). *Texts, Temples, and Traditions* [festschrift for M. Haran]. Winona Lake: Eisenbrauns, 1996, pp. 241-258.

First Speech of Yahweh (chaps. 38-39)

0384 Fox, Michael V. "Job 38 and God's Rhetoric." In John Dominic Crossan (ed.). *The Book of Job and Ricoeur's Hermeneutics* [Semeia, 19]. Chico, CA: Scholars Press, 1981, pp. 53-61.

0385 Pellauer, David. "Reading Ricoeur Reading Job." In Crossan, John Dominic (ed.). *The Book of Job and Ricoeur's Hermeneutics* [Semeia, 19]. Chico, CA: Scholars Press, 1981, pp. 73-83.

0386 Malchow, Bruce. "Nature from God's Perspective, Job 38-39." *Dialog* 21 (1982): 130-133.

0387 Rowold, Henry. "Yahweh's Challenge to Rival: The Form and Function of the Yahweh Speech in Job 38-39." *CBQ* 47 (1985): 199-211.

0388 Müller, Hans-Peter. "Die sogennante Straussenperikope in den Gottesreden des Hiobbuches." *ZAW* 100 (1988): 90-105.

0389 Miller, James E. "Structure and Meaning of the Animal Discourse in the Theophany of Job (38,3 - 39,30)." *ZAW* 103 (1991): 418-421.

0390 Crenshaw, James L. "When Form and Content Clash: The Theology of Job 38:1 - 40:5." In Richard J. Clifford and John J. Collins (eds.). *Creation in the Biblical Traditions* [CBQMS, 24]. Washington, DC: Catholic Biblical Association of America, 1992, pp. 70-84.

0391 Loader, J.A. "Seeing God with Natural Eyes: On Job and Nature." *OTE* 5/3 (1992): 346-360.

0392 Dailey, Thomas F. "Theophanic Bluster: Job and the Wind of Change." *SR* 22 (1993): 187-195.

0393 Ritter, Petra. "Die Verben des Gottesrede in Ijob 38 und 39: Eine formal-statistiche Untersuchung." In Friedrich V. Reiterer and Petrus Eder (eds.). *Liebe zum Wort: Beiträge zur klassischen und biblischen Philologie* [festschrift for L. Bernhard]. Salzburg: Otto Müller Verlag, 1993, pp. 215-237.

38

0394 Waldman, N.M. "The Heavenly Writing." *Gratz College Jewish Studies* 6 (1977): 93-97.

0395 Jamieson-Drake, David W. "Literary Structure, Genre and Interpretation in Job 38." In Kenneth Hoglund (ed.). *The Listening Heart: Essays in Wisdom and the Psalms* [festschrift for R.E. Murphy; JSOTSup, 58]. Sheffield: Academic Press, 1987, pp. 217-235.

0396 Schneider, Thomas. "Hiob 38 und die demotische Weisheit (Papyrus Insinger 24)." *TZ* 47 (1991): 108-124.

38:12-15

0397 Cornelius, Izak. "The Sun Epiphany in Job 38:12-15 and the Iconography of the Gods in the Ancient Near East - The Palestinian Connection." *JNSL* 16 (1990): 25-43.

38:28-29

0398 Vall, Gregory. "'From whose womb did the ice come forth?' Procreation Images in Job 38:28-29." *CBQ* 57 (1995): 504-513.

38:31-32

0399 Herz, N. "The Astral Terms in Job IX 9, XXXVIII 31-32." *JTS* 14 (1913): 575-577.

38:31

0400 Hess, J.-J. "Die Sternbilder in Hiob 9:9 und 38:31f." In T. Menzel (ed.). *Festschrift Georg Jacob*. Leipzig: Harrassowitz, 1932, pp. 94-99.

38:39

0401 Bezuidenhout, L.C. "Struktuur en strekking van Job 38:39 - 39:30." *HerTS* 43 (1987): 709-722.

39:5

0402 Dahood, Mitchell. "Four Ugaritic Personal Names and Job 39,5.26-27." *ZAW* 87 (1975): 220.

39:18-25

0403 Odell, David. "Images of Violence in the Horse in Job 39:18-25." *Prooftexts* 13/2 (1993): 163-173.

39:23

    0404 Borger, R. "Hiob 39,23 nach dem Qumran-Targum." *VT* 27 (1977): 102-105.

39:26-27

    0405 Dahood, Mitchell. "Four Ugaritic Personal Names and Job 39,5.26-27." *ZAW* 87 (1975): 220.

39:27-28

    0406 Driver, G.R. "Job 39:27-28. The *Ky*-Bird." *PEQ* 104 (1972): 64-66.

39:27

    0407 Grelot, P. "Note de critique textuelle sur Job xxxix 27." *VT* 22 (1972): 487-489.

Job's First Response (40:1-5)

    0408 Dailey, Thomas. "The Wisdom of Divine Disputation? On Job 40:1-5." *JSOT* 63 (1994): 105-119.

40:2

    0409 Fullerton, Kember. "On the Text and Significance of Job 40:2." *AJSL* 49 (1932-33): 197-211.

    0410 Zimmerman, Frank. "Supplementary Observations on Job 40:2." *AJSL* 51 (1934-35): 46-47.

Second Speech of Yahweh (chaps. 40:6 - 41)

    0411 Ruprecht, E. "Das Nilpferd im Hiobbuch. Beobachtungen zu der soggennante zweiten Gottesrede." *VT* 21 (1971): 209-231.

    0412 Couroyer, B. "Qui est Béhémoth?" *RB* 82 (1975): 418-445.

0413 Kinner Wilson, J.V. "A Return to the Problems of Behemoth and Leviathan." *VT* 25 (1975): 1-14.

0414 Gammie, John G. "Behemoth and Leviathan: On the Didactic and Theological Significance of Job 40:15-41:26." In J.G. Gammie, et al (eds.). *Israelite Wisdom* [festschrift for Samuel Terrien]. New York: Union Theological Seminary 1978, pp. 217-231.

0415 Young, William A. "Leviathan in the Book of Job and *Moby Dick*." *Soundings* 65 (1983): 388-401.

0416 Müller, Hans-Peter. "Die sogennante Straussenperikope in den Gottesreden des Hiobbuches." *ZAW* 100 (1988): 90-105.

0417 Wolfers, David. "Bulrush and Bramble." *JBQ* 19 (1990-91): 170-175.

0418 Wolfers, David. "The Lord's Second Speech in the Book of Job." *VT* 40 (1990): 474-499.

0419 Caquot, Andre. "Le Léviathan de Job 40,25 — 41,26." *RB* 99 (1992): 40-69.

40:6-14

0420 Gradl, Felix. "Ijobs Begegnung mit Gott: Anmerkungen zu Ijob 40,6-8.9-14." In Friedrich Reiterer (ed.). *Ein Gott, eine Offenbarung: Beiträge zur biblischen Exegese, Theologie und Spiritualität* [festschrift for Notker Füglister]. Würzburg: Echter, 1991, pp. 65-82.

40:9-14

0421 Spangenberg, I.J.J. "Om te teologiseer oor God en lyding: Opmerkings na aanleiding van Harold Kushner se interpretasie van Job 40:9-14." *HerTS* 50/4 (1994): 990-1004.

40:12

0422 Dahood, Mitchell. "*Hdk* in Job 40,12." *Bib* 49 (1968): 509.

40:14

0423   Gordis, Robert. "Job and Ecology (and the Significance of Job 40:14)." *HAR* 9 (1985): 189-202.

40:19-20

0424   Couroyer, B. "Le 'glaive' de Béhémoth, Job 40,19-20." *RB* 84 (1977): 59-79.

40:29

0425   Gordis, Robert. "Job xl 29 — An Additional Note." *VT* 14 (1964): 492-494.

41:1-4

0426   Gibson, J.C.L. "A New Look at Job 41.1-4 (English 41.9-12)." In Robert P. Carroll (ed.). *Text and Pretext* (festschrift for Robert Davidson; JSOTSup, 138). Sheffield: JSOT Press, 1992, pp. 129-139.

41:2-3

0427   Rowold, Henry. "*Mi hu'? Li hu?* Leviathan and Job in Job 41:2-3." *JBL* 105 (1986): 104-109.

41:5

0428   Herrmann, Wolfram. "Eine notwendige Erinnerung (41,5)." *ZAW* 104 (1992): 262-264.

Job's Second Response (42:1-6)

0429   Kuyper, L.J. "The Repentance of Job." *VT* 9 (1959): 91-94.

0430   Harrop, G.C. "But Now Mine Eye Seeth Thee." *CJT* 12/2 (1966): 80-84.

0431   de Wilde, A. "Jobs slotwoord." *NedTTs* 32 (1978): 265-269.

0432 Curtis, John Briggs. "On Job's Response to Yahweh." *JBL* 98 (1979): 497-511.

0433 Newell, B.L. "Job: Repentant or Rebellious?" *WTJ* 46 (1984): 298-316.

0434 Tilley, Terrence. "God and the Silencing of Job." *Modern Theology* 5 (1989): 257-270.

0435 Shelley, John C. "Job 42:1-6 — God's Bet and Job's Repentance." *RevExp* 89 (1992): 541-546.

0436 van Wolde, E.J. "Job 42,1-6: The Reversal of Job." In W. Beuken (ed.). *The Book of Job* [BETL, 114]. Leuven: University Press, 1994, pp. 223-250.

42:2-3

0437 Dailey, Thomas F. "'Wondrously far from me'— The Wisdom of Job 42,2-3." *BZ* 36 (1992): 261-264.

42:3

0438 Bergant, Dianne. "Things Too Wonderful for Me (Job 42:3)." In Carolyn Osiek and Donald Senior (eds.). *Scripture and Prayer* [festschrift for Carroll Stuhlmueller]. Wilmington: Glazier, 1988, pp. 62-75.

42:6

0439 Patrick, Dale. "The Translation of Job xlii 6." *VT* 26 (1976): 369-371.

0440 Kaplan, L.J. "Maimonides, Dale Patrick and Job xlii 6." *VT* 28 (1978): 356-358.

0441 O'Connor, Daniel J. "Job's Final Word - 'I Am Consoled' (42:6*b*)." *ITQ* 50 (1983-84): 181-197.

0442 Morrow, W. "Consolation, Rejection, and Repentance in Job 42:6." *JBL* 105 (1986): 211-225.

0443 Muenchow, C. "Dust and Dirt in Job 42:6." *JBL* 108 (1989): 597-611.

0444 Wolters, A. "A Child of Dust and Ashes? (Job 42,6*b*)." *ZAW* 102 (1990): 116-119.

0445 de Boer, P.A.H. "Does Job Retract? Job xlii,6." In C. van Duin (ed.). *Selected Studies in Old Testament Exegesis* [OTS, 27]. Leiden: Brill, 1991, pp. 179-195.

0446 Dailey, Thomas F. "And Yet He Repents — On Job 42,6." *ZAW* 105 (1993): 205-209.

EPILOGUE (42:7-17)

0447 Fullerton, Kember. "The Original Conclusion to the Book of Job." *ZAW* 42 (1924): 116-135.

0448 Batten, L.W. "The Epilogue of the Book of Job." *ATR* 15 (1933): 125-128.

0449 Williams, James G. "'You have not spoken truth of me' - Mystery and Irony in Job." *ZAW* 83 (1971): 231-255.

0450 Nakazawa, Koki. "On the Dénouement of the Joban Poem." *Kirisutokyo Gaku* 19 (1977): 1-17.

0451 Forrest, Robert. "An Inquiry into Yahweh's Commendation of Job." *SR* 9 (1979): 159-168.

0452 Kaiser, Otto. "Ijob's Abrechnung mit den Freunden." *BK* 46 (1991): 159-164.

0453 Pyper, Hugh. "The Reader in Pain: Job as Text and Pretext." In Robert Carroll (ed.). *Text and Pretext* [festschrift for Robert Davidson; JSOTSup, 138]. Sheffield: JSOT Press, 1992, pp. 234-255.

0453a Mathew, Geevarughese. "The Role of the Epilogue in the Book of Job." Dissertation, Drew University, 1995.

42:7-10

0454 Cimosa, Mario. "L'intercessione di Giobbe in LXX Gb 42,7-10." *Salesianum* 48 (1986): 513-538.

42:7-9

0455 Wagner, Siegfried. "Theologischer Versuch über Ijob 42,7-9." In Jutta Jausmann and Hans-Jürgen Zobel (eds.). *Alttestamentliche Glaube und Biblische Theologie* [festschrift for Horst Dietrich Preuß]. Stuttgart: Kohlhammer, 1992, pp. 216-224.

42:7

0456 Freund, Yosef. "'For You Have Not Spoken Correctly of Me As Has My Servant Job' (Job 42:7)." *Beth Mikra* 34 (1989-90): 124-130.

0457 O'Connor, Daniel J. "The Cunning Hand: Repetitions in Job 42:7,8." *ITQ* 57 (1991): 14-25.

0458 Porter, Stanley E. "The Message of the Book of Job: Job 42:7*b* as Key to Interpretation?" *EvQ* 63 (1991): 291-304.

42:13-15

0459 Lesses, Rebecca. "The Daughters of Job." In Elisabeth Schüssler Fiorenza (ed.). *Searching the Scriptures: A Feminist Commentary*, vol.II. New York: Crossroad, 1994, pp. 139-149

Part Two

Citations by SUBJECT

Afterlife
Anthropology

Biblical Literature - Job & Abraham
Biblical Literature - Job & Amos
Biblical Literature - Job & Ben Sira
Biblical Literature - Job & Isaiah
Biblical Literature - Job & Jacob
Biblical Literature - Job & Jeremiah
Biblical Literature - Job & Jonah
Biblical Literature - Job & Moses
Biblical Literature - Job & Proverbs
Biblical Literature - Job & Qoheleth
Biblical Literature - Job & Song of Songs

Chaos

Characterization - the Friends
Characterization - God
Characterization - JOB
Characterization - Satan
Characterization - the Wife

Comparative Literature
Comparative Literature - Ancient Near East
Comparative Literature - Greek
Comparative Literature - Modern

Creation

Death

Ethics
Evil

Faith
Fear of God

Genre (form)
God-Question

History of Interpretation - Patristic
History of Interpretation - Medieval
History of Interpretation - Rabbinic
History of Interpretation - Reformation
History of Interpretation - Jewish
History of Interpretation - Christian
History of Interpretation - Modern

Holiness
Hope

Iconography

Intertextuality
Intertextuality - Torah
Intertextuality - Historical
Intertextuality - Prophets
Intertextuality - Writings

Justice

Language
Literary

Motifs
Motifs - irony/parody
Motifs - law
Motifs - metaphor
Motifs - mythology

Narrativity
New Testament References

Pastoral Concerns
Pastoral Concerns - Preaching
Pastoral Concerns - Teaching

Philology
Philology - Northwest Semitic
Philology - Ugaritic

Philosophy
Politics
Prayer
Psychology

Religion
Repentance
Rhetoric

Science
Septuagint
Sin
Social Studies
Soteriology
Spirituality
Structure
Suffering

Targums
Testament of Job
Theodicy
Theology

Wisdom

Afterlife

0460 Garcia Cordero, M. "La tesis de la sanción moral y la esperanza de la recurrección en el libro de Job." In *La encíclica Humani Generis* [XII Semaña Bíblica Española]. Madrid: Libreria Cientifica Medinaceli, 1952, pp. 571-594.

0461 Garcia Cordero, M. "La esperanza de la recurrección corporal en Job." *Ciencia Tomista* 80 (1953): 1-23.

0462 Gard, D.H. "The Concept of the Future Life according to the Greek Translator of the Book of Job." *JBL* 73 (1954): 137-143.

0463 Benamozegh, E. "L'immortalità dell'anima in Giobbe e nei Proverbi." *Annali di Storia Ebraica* 8 (1977): 145-172.

0464 Mintingh, L.M. "Life, Death and Resurrection in the Book of Job." In W.C. van Wyk (ed.). *Old Testament Essays: Studies in the Pentateuch*. Pretoria: University Department of Semitic Languages, 1977, pp. 32-44.

0465 Althann, R. "Job and the Idea of the Beatific Afterlife." *OTE* 4 (1991): 316-326.

0466 Coggi, Roberto. "La prova morale dell'immortalità dell'anima nel commento di S. Tommaso al libro di Giobbe." *Divus Thomas* 95,1 (1992): 157-163.

Anthropology

0467 Thelen, Mary Frances. "*J.B.*, Job, and the Biblical Doctrine of Man." *JBR* 27 (1959): 201-205.

0468 Bergant, Dianne. "An Historico-Critical Study of the Anthropological Traditions and Motifs in Job." Dissertation, St. Louis University, 1975.

0469 Eising, H. In J.B. von Bauer (ed.). *Das Menschenleben im Buch Ijob* [festschrift for F. Sauer]. Graz 1977, pp. 43-57.

0470 Barron, Mary Catherine. "Sitting It Out with Job: The Human Condition." *Review for Religious* 38 (1979): 489-496.

0471   Habel, Norman. "'Naked I Came ...'; Humanness in the Book of Job." In J. Jeremias und L. Perlitt (eds.). *Die Botschaft und die Boten* [festschrift for H. Walter Wolff]. Neukerchen-Vluyn, 1981, pp. 373-392.

0472   Pifano, P. "Nel grido di Giobbe il grido dell'uomo contemporaneo." *Asprenas* 31 (1984): 497-524.

0473   Fohrer, Georg. "Man and Disease According to the Book of Job." *Koroth* 9 (1987): 43-48.

0474   Gemuyt, François. "Job et la condition humaine." *Sémiotique et Bible* 56 (1989): 37-41.

0475   Tortolone, Gian Michele. "L'enigma di Giobbe. Destino dell'uomo e silenzio di Dio." *Asprenas* 36 (1989): 22-38.

0476   Remus, Martin. *Menschenbildvorstellungen im Ijob-Buch: Ein Beitrag zur alttestamentlichen Anthropologie* [BEATAJ, 21]. Frankfurt am Main: Lang, 1993.

Biblical Literature - Job & Abraham

0477   Shapiro, D.S. "The Book of Job and the Trial of Abraham." *Tradition* 4 (1962): 210-220.

0478   Oberforcher, Robert. "Abraham, Jeremia, Ijob: Typen des von Gott beanspruchten Menschen." *BLit* 52 (1979): 183-191.

0479   Schreiner, Stefan. "Der gotesfürchtige Rebell." *ZTK* 89/2 (1992): 159-171.

0480   Weinberg, J. "Job versus Abraham: The Quest for the Perfect God-Fearer in Rabbinic Tradition." In W. Beuken (ed.), *The Book of Job* [BETL, 114]. Leuven: University Press, 1994, pp. 281-296.

Biblical Literature - Job & Amos

0481 Crenshaw, James L. "The Influence of the Wise upon Amos: The 'Doxologies of Amos' and Job 5,9-16; 9,5-10." *ZAW* 79 (1967): 42-52.

Biblical Literature - Job & Ben Sira

0482 Reiterer, F.V. "Das Verhältnis Ijobs und Ben Siras." In W. Beuken (ed.), *The Book of Job* [BETL, 114]. Leuven: University Press, 1994, pp. 405-429.

Biblical Literature - Job & Isaiah

0483 Camhy, O. *Une trilogie biblique sur le drame de la vie: un sujet, trois conceptions.* Paris: Grassin, 1973.

0484 Andre, Gunnel. "Deuterojesaja och Jobsboken: en jamforande studie." *SEÅ* 54 (1989): 33-42.

0485 Curtis, John Briggs. "Elihu and Deutero-Isaiah: A Study in Literary Dependence." *PEGLMBS* 10 (1990): 31-38.

0486 de la Fuente, Alfonso. "Job y el Siervo de Yahvé: dos interpretacione del sufrimento." In Manuel Gesteira Garza (ed.). *Dios y el problema del mal* [Actas de la 3ª Semana de Teología]. *Revista Española de Teología* 51 (1991): 237-251.

Biblical Literature - Job & Jacob

0487 Davis, E.F. "Job and Jacob: The Integrity of Faith." In Danna Nolan Fewell (ed.). *Reading Between Texts:* Intertextuality and the Hebrew Bible [Literary Currents in Biblical Interpretation]. Louisville: Westminster/John Knox, 1992, pp. 203-224.

Biblical Literature - Job & Jeremiah

0488 Fishbane, M. "Jeremiah iv 23-26 and Job iii 3-13: A Recovered Use of the Creation Pattern." *VT* 21 (1971): 151-167.

0489   Vinton, Patricia. "Radical Aloneness: Job and Jeremiah." *TBT* 99 (1978): 1843-1849.

0490   Oberforcher, Robert. "Abraham, Jeremia, Ijob: Typen des von Gott beanspruchten Menschen." *BLit* 52 (1979): 183-191.

0491   McDonagh, Kathleen. "Job and Jeremiah: Their Approach to God." *TBT* 18 (1980): 331-335.

0492   Burns, John Barclay. "Cursing the Day of Birth." *PEGLMBS* 13 (1993): 11-22.

Biblical Literature - Job & Jonah

0493   Vawter, Bruce. *Job and Jonah: Questioning the Hidden God.* New York: Paulist Press, 1983.

Biblical Literature - Job & Moses

0494   Ceresko, Anthony. "Surrender (?) to God in the Old Testament: Some Reflections on Moses and Job." *Indian Journal of Spirituality* 7/2 (1994): 168-181.

Biblical Literature - Job & Proverbs

0495   Holmgrew, Frederick. "Barking Dogs Never Bite, Except Now and Then: Proverbs and Job." *ATR* 61/3 (1979): 341-353.

Biblical Literature - Job & Qoheleth

0496   Camhy, O. *Une trilogie biblique sur le drame de la vie: un sujet, trois conceptions.* Paris: Grassin, 1973.

0497   Loader, J.A. "Different Reactions of Job and Qoheleth to the Doctrine of Retribution." In W. Wyk (ed.). *Studies in Wisdom Literature* [Ou-Testamentiese Werkgemeenskap In Suider-Afrika, 15]. Hercules, SA: NHW Press, 1981, pp. 43-48.

0498 Crüsemann, Frank. "Hiob und Kohelet: Ein Beitrag zum Verständnis des Hiobbuches." In R. Albertz, H.-P. Müller, H.W. Wolff, and W. Zimmerli (eds.). *Werden und Wirken des Alten Testaments* [festschrift for C. Westermann]. Göttingen: Vandenhoeck & Ruprecht, 1980, pp. 373-393.

0499 Whybray, R.N. *Two Jewish Theologies: Job and Ecclesiastes.* Hull 1980.

0500 Festorazzi, Franco. "Giobbe e Qohelet: crisi della sapienza." In Rinaldo Fabris (ed.). *Problemi e prospettive di scienze bibliche.* Brescia: Queriniana, 1981, pp. 233-258.

0501 Maggioni, Bruno. *Giobbe e Qohelet: la contestazione sapienziale nella Bibbia.* Assisi: Cittadella, 1989.

0502 Robertson, David. "Job and Ecclesiastes." *Soundings* 73 (1990): 257-272.

0503 Newsom, Carol A. "Job and Ecclesiastes." In James L. Mays, et. al. (eds). *Old Testament Interpretation: Past, Present and Future* [festschrift for Gene M. Tucker]. Nashville: Abingdon, 1995, pp. 177-194.

Biblical Literature - Job & Song of Songs

0504 Paul, S.M. "An Unrecognized Medical Idiom in Canticles 6,12 and Job 9,21." *Bib* 59 (1978): 545-547.

0505 Cook, A. *The Root of the Thing: A Study of Job and the Song of Songs.* Bloomington: Indiana University Press, 1968.

Chaos

0506 Cepeda Calzada, P. "El Leviatán, símbolo bíblico: El Caos frente a la idea de ley en Job." *Crisis* 21 (1974): 219-268.

0507 Nel, P.J. "Cosmos and Chaos: A Reappraisal of the Divine Discourses in the Book of Job." *OTE* 4 (1991): 206-226.

0508   Fuchs, Gisela. "Der Mythos vom Chaoskampf in der Hiobdichtung: Rezeption und Umdeutung einer altorientalischen Tradition." Dissertation, Bonn, 1992.

0509   Yeager, Janet and Thomas Dailey. "Job's World: A Chaotic Conundrum!" *Encounter* 56/2 (1995): 175-187.

Characterization - the Friends

0510   Albright, W.F. "The Name of Bildad the Shuhite." *AJSL* 44 (1927-28): 31-36.

0511   Speiser, E.A. "On the Name of Bildad." *JAOS* 49 (1929): 360.

0512   Habel, Norman. "'Only the jackal is my friend': On Friends and Redeemers in Job." *Int* 31 (1977): 227-236.

0513   Clines, David J.A. "The Arguments of Job's Three Friends." In David J.A. Clines, David M. Gunn, and Alan J. Hauser (eds.). *Art and Meaning: Rhetoric in Biblical Literature* [JSOTSup, 19]. Sheffield: Almond Press, 1982, pp. 199-214.

0514   Lévêque, Jean. "Tradition and Betrayal in the Speeches of the Friends." In C. Duquoc and C. Floristan (eds.). *Job and the Silence of God* [Concilium, 169]. Edinburgh: T&T Clark, 1983, pp. 39-44.

0515   Littleton, Mark R. "Where Job's 'Comforters' Went Wrong." In Roy B. Zuck (ed.). *Sitting with Job: Selected Studies on the Book of Job*. Grand Rapids: Baker, 1992, pp. 253-260.

0516   Freund, Yosef. "Were Job's Friends Gentiles?" *Dor le Dor* 18 1989-90): 107-110.

0517   Albertz, Rainer. "The Sage and Pious Wisdom in the Book of Job: The Friends' Perspective." In John G. Gammie and Leo G. Perdue (eds.). *The Sage in Israel and the Ancient Near East*. Winona Lake: Eerdmans, 1990, pp. 243-261.

0518   Kisch, Jeremy. "Job's Friends: Psychotherapeutic Precursors in the Ancient Near East." *Psychotherapy* 27/1 (1990): 46-52

0519 Kutsch, Ernst. "Hiob und seine Freunde: zu Problemen der Rahmenerzählung des Hiobbuches." In Siegfried Jreuzer and Kurt Lüthi (eds.). *Zur Aktualität des Alten Testaments* [festschrift for Georg Sauer]. Frankfurt am Main: Lang, 1992, pp. 73-83.

0520 Simundson, Daniel J. "Job and His Ministers." In Arland J. Hultgren, et al. (eds.). *All Things New* [festschrift for Roy A. Harrisville; Word and World Supplement Series, 1]. St. Paul: Word and World, 1992, pp. 33-42.

0520a O'Connor, Donal J. *Job: His Wife, His Friends, and His God.* Dublin: Columbia Press, 1995.

Characterization - God

0521 Berg, Werner. "Gott und der Gerechte in der Rahmenerzählung des Buches Job." *MTZ* 32 (1981): 206-221.

0522 Kinet, Dirk. "The Ambiguity of the Concepts of God and Satan in the Book of Job." In C. Duquoc and C. Floristan (eds.). *Job and the Silence of God* [Concilium, 169]. Edingurgh: T&T Clark, 1983, pp. 30-38.

0523 Nielsen, Eduard. "*Shadday* in the Book of Job." In Egon Keck, et al. (eds.). *Living Waters: Scandanavian Orientalistic Studies* [festschrift for F. Løkkegaard]. Kopenhagen: Musuem Tusculanum, 1990, pp. 249-258.

0524 Habel, Norman C. "In Defense of God the Sage." In Leo G. Perdue and W. Clark Gilpin (eds.). *The Voice from the Whirlwind: Interpreting the Book of Job.* Nashville: Abingdon, 1992, pp. 21-38.

0525 Mettinger, Tryggve N.D. "The God of Job: Avenger, Tyrant, or Victor?" In Leo G. Perdue and W. Clark Gilpin (eds.). *The Voice from the Whirlwind: Interpreting the Book of Job.* Nashville: Abingdon, 1992, pp. 39-49.

0526 Williams, James G. "Job and the God of Victims." In Leo G. Perdue and W. Clark Gilpin (eds.). *The Voice from the Whirlwind: Interpreting the Book of Job.* Nashville: Abingdon, 1992, pp. 208-231.

0527 Handy, Lowell K. "The Authorization of Divine Power and the Guilt of God in the Book of Job: Useful Ugaritic Parallels." *JSOT* 60 (1993): 107-118.

0528 Janzen, J. Gerald. "On the Moral Nature of God's Power: Yahweh and the Sea in Job and Deutero-Isaiah." *CBQ* 56/3 (1994): 458-478.

0529 Spieckermann, Hermann. "Die Satanisierungen Gottes: Zur inneren Konkordanz von Novelle, Dialoge und Gottesreden im Hiobbuch." In Ingo Kottsieper, et al. (eds.). *"Wer ist wie deu, HERR, unter den Göttern?" Studien zur Theologie und Religionsgeschichte* [festschrift for O. Kaiser]. Göttingen: Vandenhoech und Ruprecht, 1994, pp. 431-444.

0530 Strauß, Hans. "Bemerkungen zu Gebrauch und Bedeutung von אל in der Hiobdichtung und Gesamtkomposition." In Peter Mommer and Winfried Thiel (eds.). *Altes Testament Forschung und Wirkung* [festschrift for Henning Graf Reventlow]. Frankfurt am Main: Peter Lang, 1994, pp. 95-101.

0530a O'Connor, Donal J. *Job: His Wife, His Friends, and His God.* Dublin: Columbia Press, 1995.

Characterization - Job

0531 McKechnie, James. *Job: Moral Hero, Religious Egoist and Mystic.* New York: Doran, 1927.

0532 Steinberg, Milton. "Job Answers God: Being the Religious Perplexities of an Obscure Pharisee." *JR* 12/2 (1932): 159-176.

0533 Brown, M. Webster. "Was Job a Leper?" *Medical Journal and Record* (July 1933): 32-33.

0534 Brim, Charles. "Job's Illness — Pellagra." *Archives of Dermatology and Syphilology* 46/2 (Feb 1942): 371-376.

0535 Neher, André. "L'homme biblique, Job." *L'existence juive.* Paris 1962, pp. 63-72.

0536 Bonnard, P.E. "Job ou l'homme enfin exstasié." *LumVie* 13 (1964): 15-33.

0537 Bloch, Ernst. "L'uomo Giobbe." *De Homine* 24 (1967): 3-18.

0538 Israel, S. "Hiob: Prometheus in Judäa." *Antaios* 9 (1967): 369-384.

0539 Ginsberg, H.L. "Job the Patient and Job the Impatient." In J.A. Emerton (ed.). *Congress Volume* [VTSup, 17]. Leiden: Brill, 1969, pp. 88-111.

0540 Bonora, A. *Il contestatore di Dio: Giobbe*. Torino: Marietti, 1978.

0541 Goldschmidt, H.L. "Hiob einst und immer." In Gotthold Müller (ed.). *Israel hat dennoch Gott zum Trost* [festschrift for Ben-Chroin Schalom]. Trier: Paulinus, 1978, pp. 20-30.

0542 Gramlich, Miriam Louise. "Job — Before and After." *TBT* 94 (February 1978): 1494-1502.

0543 Jason, Heda. "The Poor Man from Nippur: an Ethnopoetic Analysis." *JCS* 31 (1979): 189-215.

0544 MacKenzie, R.A.F. "The Transformation of Job." *BTB* 9 (1979): 51-57.

0545 Rauchwarger, J. "Antonio Enríquez Gómez: *Epistolas tres de Job*. A Matter of Racial Atavism?" *REJ* 138 (1979): 69-87.

0546 de Pury, R. *Job ou l'homme révolté* [Essais bibliques, 4]. Geneva: Labor et Fides, 1982.

0547 Dedmon, Robert. "Job as Holocaust Survivor." *St. Luke's Journal of Theology* 26 (1982): 165-185.

0548 Moore, Rick D. "The Integrity of Job." *CBQ* 45 (1983): 17-31.

0549 Nash, J. "Images of Job." *Review for Religious* 42 (1983): 28-33.

0550 Westermann, Claus. "The Two Faces of Job." In C. Duquoc and C. Floristan (eds.). *Job and the Silence of God* [Concilium, 169]. Edinburgh: T&T Clark, 1983, pp. 15-22.

0551 Southwick, Jay. "Job: An Exemplar for All Ages." *Encounter* 45 (1984): 373-391.

0552 Girard, René. "'The Ancient Trail Trodden by the Wicked': Job as Scapegoat." *Semeia* 33 (1985): 13-41.

0553 Girard, René. *La route antique des hommes pervers.* Paris: Grasset & Fasquelle, 1985.

0554 Levine, Baruch. "Rene Girard on Job: The Question of the Scapegoat." *Semeia* 33 (1985): 125-133.

0555 O'Connor, Daniel J. "Reverence or Irreverence in Job." *ITQ* 51 (1985): 85-104.

0556 Ortiz de Urtaran, Felix. "Un rico amigo de dios." *Lumen* 34 (1985): 289-313.

0557 Wolfers, David. "Is Job After All Jewish?" *Dor le Dor* 14 (1985): 39-44.

0558 Christensen, D. "Job and the Age of the Patriarchs in the Old Testament." *Perspectives in Religious Studies* 13 (1986): 225-228.

0559 Miller, Ward S. "Job, Creator's Apprentice." *Chicago Studies* 26 (1987): 166-177.

0560 Forrest, Robert. "The Two Faces of Job: Imagery and Integrity in the Prologue." In L. Eslinger and G. Taylor (eds.). *Ascribe to the Lord* [festschrift for P.C. Craigie; JSOTSup, 67]. Sheffield: Almond Press, 1988, pp. 385-398.

0561 Jeremias, Jörg. "Hiob der Rebell und Hiob der Gaheltene." *Katechetische Blätter* 113 (1988): 592-598.

0562 Brenner, Athalya. "'Job the Pious': The Characterization of Job in the Narrative Framework of the Book." *JSOT* 43 (1989): 37-52.

0563 O'Connor, Daniel J. "The Hybris of Job." *ITQ* 55 (1989): 125-141.

0564 Bergant, Dianne. "Might Job Have Been a Feminist?" *TBT* 28 (1990): 342-346.

0565 Terrien, Samuel. "Job as a Sage." In John G. Gammie and Leo G. Perdue (eds.). *The Sage in Israel and the Ancient Near East*. Winona Lake: Eerdmans, 1990, pp. 231-242.

0566 Reiser, W. *Hiob: Ein Rebell bekommt Recht*. Stuttgart: Quell, 1991.

0567 Wittenberg, G.H. "Job the Farmer: the Judean *'am ha-arez* and the Wisdom Movement." *OTE* 4 (1991): 151-170.

0568 Calati, Benedetto, et. al. *Le provocazioni di Giobbe: una figura biblical nell'orizzonte letterario* [Punti critici, 1]. Genova: Marietti, 1992.

0569 Gavaler, Campion P. "The Transformation of Job." *TBT* 30,4 (1992): 208-212.

0570 Girard, Réne. "Job as Failed Scapegoat." In Leo G. Perdue and W. Clark Gilpin (eds.). *The Voice from the Whilrwind: Interpreting the Book of Job*. Nashville: Abingdon Press, 1992, pp. 185-207.

0571 Wolfers, David. "Job: A Universal Drama." *JBQ* 21 (1993): 13-23, 80-89.

0572 Begg, C.T. "Comparing Characters: The Book of Job and the *Testament of Job*." In W. Beuken (ed.), *The Book of Job* [BETL, 114]. Leuven: University Press, 1994, pp. 435-445.

0573 Dailey, Thomas F. *The Repentant Job: A Ricoeurian Icon for Biblical Theology*. Lanham, MD: University Press of America, 1994.

0574 Day, J. "How Could Job Be an Edomite?" In W. Beuken (ed.), *The Book of Job* [BETL, 114]. Leuven: University Press, 1994, pp. 392-399.

0575 Holm-Nielsen, S. "Is Job a Scapegoat?" In *Festschrift B. Otzen*, 1994, pp. 128-135.

0576 Cheney, Michael. *Dust, Wind and Agony: Character, Speech and Genre in Job* [ConBOT, 36]. Stockholm: Almqvist and Wiksell, 1995.

0577 Wolfers, David. "The Book of Job: Its True Significance." *JBQ* 24 (1996): 3-8.

0578 Dailey, Thomas F. "Job as an Icon for Theology." *Perspectives in Religious Studies* 23/3 (1997): n.p.

Characterization - Satan

0579 Kinet, Dirk. "The Ambiguity of the Concepts of God and Satan in the Book of Job." In C. Duquoc and C. Floristan (eds.). *Job and the Silence of God* [Concilium, 169]. Edinburgh: T&T Clark, 1983, pp. 30-38.

0580 Gammie, John G. "The Angelology and Demonology in the Septuagint of the Book of Job." *HUCA* 56 (1985): 1-19.

0581 Levin, S. "Satan: Psychologist." *Dor le Dor* 18 (1989-90): 157-164.

0582 Rahman, Yosefa. "The Satan in the Book of Job." *Beth Mikra* 35/123 (1990): 334-340.

0583 Nielsen, Kirsten. "Whatever Became of You, Satan? or a Literary-Critical Analysis of the Role of Satan in the Book of Job." In Klaus D. Schunck and Matthias Augustin (eds.). *Goldene Apfel in silbernen Schalen* [XII Congress of the International Organization for the Study of the Old Testament]. Frankfurt am Main: Peter Lang, 1992, pp. 129-134.

0584 Grayston, Kenneth. "Satan and Job." *ScrB* 23 (1993): 2-7.

0585 Handy, Lowell, K. "The Authorization of Divine Power and the Guilt of God in the Book of Job: Useful Ugaritic Parallels." *JSOT* 60 (1993): 107-118.

Characterization - the Wife

0585a West, Gerald. "Hearing Job's Wife." *OTE* 4 (1991): 107-131.

0585b Gitay, Zefira. "The Portrayal of Job's Wife and Her Representation in the Visual Arts." In Astrid B. Beck, et al. (eds.). *Fortunate the Eyes that See* [festschrift for D.N. Freedman]. Grand Rapids: Eerdmans, 1995, pp. 516-526.

0585c O'Connor, Donal J. *Job: His Wife, His Friends, and His God.* Dublin: Columbia Press, 1995.

Comparative Literature

0586 Murtagh, J. "The Book of of Job and the Book of the Dead." *ITQ* 35 (1968): 166-173.

0587 Rao, S. Prabhakara and M. Reddy. "Job and His Satan - Parallels in Indian Scripture." *ZAW* 91 (1979): 416-422.

0588 O'Connor, Daniel J. "The Keret Legend and the Prologue-Epilogue of Job." *ITQ* 55 (1989): 1-6.

0589 Blumenthal, Elke. "Hiob und die Harfnerlieder." *TLZ* 115/10 (1990): 721-730.

0590 Fontaine, Carole R. "Wounded Hero or a Shaman's Quest: Job in the Context of Folk Literature." In Leo G. Perdue and W. Clark Gilpin (eds.). *The Voice from the Whirlwind: Interpreting the Book of Job.* Nashville: Abingdon, 1992, 70-85.

0591 Laeuchli, S. and A. Sharma. "The Problem of Job: An Eastern Response." *ARC* (Journal of the Faculty of Religious Studies, McGill University) 22 (1994): 83-90.

Comparative Literature - Ancient Near East

0592 Gray, J. "The Book of Job in the Context of Near Eastern Literature." *ZAW* 82 (1970): 251-269.

0593 Negoiță, Athanasie. "Un Iov babilonean? Ceva din teodiceea akkadiana." *Studii Teologice* (1977): 436-449.

0594 Preuß, Horst Dietrich. "Jahwes Antwort an Hiob und die sogennannte Hiob-literatur des alten Vorderen Orients." In H. Donner, R. Hanhart and R. Smend (eds.). *Beiträge zur alttestamentlichen Theologie* [festschrift for W. Zimmerli]. Göttingen: Vandenhoeck, 1977, pp. 323-343.

0595 Müller, Hans-Peter. "Keilschriftliche Parallelen zum biblischen Hiobbuch: Möglichkeit und Grenze des Vergleichs." *Or* 47 (1978): 360-375.

0596 Müller, Hans-Peter. *Das Hiobproblem: Seine Stellung und Entstehung im Alten Orient und im Alten Testament* [ErFor, 84]. Darmstadt 1978.

0597 Albertz, Rainer. "Der sozialgeschichtliche Hintergrund des Hiobbuches und der 'Babylonische Theodizee'." In J. Jeremias and L. Perlitt (eds.). *Die Botschaft und die Boten* [festschrift for Hans Walter Wolff]. Neukerchen-Vluyn, 1981, pp. 349-372.

0598 Albertson, R.G. "Job and Ancient Near East Wisdom Literature." In W.H. Hallo, J.C. Moyer, and L.G. Perdue (eds.). *Scripture in Context, II:* More Essays on the Comparative Method. Winona Lake: Eisenbrauns, 1983, pp. 213-230.

0599 Weinfeld, M. "Job and Its Mesopotamian Parallels — A Typological Analysis." In W. Claassen (ed.). *Text and Context* [JSOTSup, 48]. Sheffield: JSOT Press, 1988, pp. 217-226.

0600 Cornelius, Izak. "The Sun Epiphany in Job 38:12-15 and the Iconography of the Gods in the Ancient Near East - The Palestinian Connection." *JNSL* 16 (1990): 25-43.

0601 Mattingly, Gerald L. "The Pious Sufferer: Mesopotamia's Traditional Theodicy and Job's Counselors." In William Hallo, Bruce Jones, and Gerald Mattingly (eds). *The Bible in the Light of Cuneiform Literature*. Lewiston, NY: Edwin Mellen, 1990, pp. 305-348.

0602 Hoffman, Yair. "Ancient Near Eastern Literary Conventions and the Restoration of the Book of Job." *ZAW* 103 (1991): 399-411.

0603 Fuchs, Gisela. "Der Mythos vom Chaoskampf in der Hiobdichtung: Rezeption und Umdeutung einer altorientalischen Tradition." Dissertation, Bonn, 1992.

0604 Müller, H.-P. "Die Hiobrahmenerzählung und ihre altorientalischen Parallelen als Paradigmen einer weisheitlichen Wirklichkeitswahrnahme." In W. Beuken (ed.), *The Book of Job* [BETL, 114]. Leuven: University Press, 1994, pp. 21-40.

Comparative Literature - Greek

0605 Israel, S. "Hiob: Prometheus in Judäa." *Antaios* 9 (1967): 369-384.

0606 Murray, G. "Prometheus and Job." In P.S. Sanders (ed.). *Twentieth Century Interpretations of the Book of Job: A Collection of Critical Essays.* Englewood Cliffs: Prentice-Hall, 1968, pp. 56-65.

Comparative Literature - Modern

0607 Thelen, Mary Frances. "*J.B.*, Job, and the Biblical Doctrine of Man." *JBR* 27 (1959): 201-205.

0608 Francisco, N.A. "Job in World Literature." *Review and Expositor* 68/4 (1971): 521-533.

0609 Schubert, Beatrix. "Vom Umgang mit demmenschlichen Leiden: ein Versuch über Ijob in der modernen Literatur." *Erbe und Auftrag* 60 (1984): 356-375.

0610 Priest, John. "Job and *J.B.*: The Goodness of God or the Godness of Good." *Horizons* 12/2 (1985): 265-283.

0611 Barge, Laura. "Job's Travail of Creation in Hokpins' Poetry. *Cithara* 31/1 (1991): 36-45.

0612 Lasine, Stuart. "Job and His Friends in the Modern World: Kafka's *The Trial*." In Leo G. Perdue and W. Clark Gilpin (eds.). *The Voice from the Whirlwind: Interpreting the Book of Job.* Nashville: Abingdon Press, 1992, pp. 144-145.

Creation

0613 Fishbane, M. "Jeremiah iv 23-26 and Job iii 3-13: A Recovered Use of the Creation Pattern." *VT* 21 (1971): 151-167.

0614 Schmidt, Paul. "Sinnfrage und Glaubenskrise: Ansätze zu einer kritischen Theologie der Schöpfung im Buche Hiob." *Geist und Leben* 45 (1972): 348-363.

0615 Forrest, R.W.E. "The Creation Motif in the Book of Job." Dissertation, MacMaster University, 1975.

0616 Möller, M. "Die Gerechtigkeit Gottes des Schöpfers in der Erfahrung seines Knechtes Hiob." *Theologische Versuche* 6 (1975): 25-36.

0617 Rowold, H.J. "The Theology of Creation in the Yahweh Speeches of the Book of Job as a Solution to the Problem Posed by the Book of Job." Dissertation, Concordia Seminary in Exile (Chicago), 1977.

0618 Wagner, Siegfried. "'Schöpfung' im Buche Hiob." *Die Zeichen der Zeit* 34 (1980): 93-96.

0619 Malchow, Bruce. "Nature from God's Perspective, Job 38-39." *Dialog* 21 (1982): 130-133.

0620 Harris, Scott L. "Wisdom or Creation? A New Interpretation of Job." *VT* 33 (1983): 419-427.

0621 Gordis, Robert. "Job and Ecology (and the Significance of Job 40:14)." *HAR* 9 (1985): 189-202.

0622 Perdue, Leo G. "Job's Assault on Creation." *HAR* 10 (1986): 295-315.

0623 Janzen, J. Gerald. "Creation and the Human Predicament in Job 1:9-11 and 38-41." *Ex Auditu* 3 (1987): 45-53.

0624 Lévêque, Jean. "L'argument de la création dans le livre de Job." In *La Création dans l'Orient Ancien* [Congrès de l'ACFEB, 1985; LD, 127]. Paris: Cerf, 1987, pp. 261-299.

0625 Loader, J.A. "Seeing God with Natural Eyes: On Job and Nature." *OTE* 5/3 (1992): 346-360.

0626 Greenhalgh, Stephen. "Waiting for God's *'oth.*" *ScrB* 23 (1993): 39-41.

0627 McKibben, Bill. *The Comforting Wind: God, Job, and the Scale of Creation.* Grand Rapids: Eerdmans, 1994.

0628 Bergant, Dianne. "The Integrity of All Creation." *TBT* 33 (1995): 5-8.

Death

0629 Crumbach, K.H. "Splitter zum Problem des Todes." *Geist und Leben* 43 (1970): 325-338.

0630 Michel, Walter L. "Death in Job." *Dialog* 11/3 (1972): 183-189.

0631 Long, Thomas J. "Life After Death: the Biblical View." *TBT* 20 (1982): 347-353.

0632 Perani, Mauro. "Giobbe di fronte alla morte." In D. Giuseppe (ed.). *Gesù e la sua morte* [Atti della XXVII Settimana Biblica]. Brescia: Paideia, 1984, pp. 267-291.

0633 Smith, David L. "The Concept of Death in Job and Ecclesiastes." *Didaskalia* 4/1 (1992): 2-14.

Ethics

0634 Faur, J. "Reflections on Job and Situation Morality." *Judaism* 19 (1970): 219-225.

0635 Osswald, E. "Hiob 31 im Rahmen der alttestamentliche Ethik." In J. Rogge (ed.). *Theologische Versuche.* Berlin: 1970, pp. 9-26.

0636 Stockhammer, M. "Theorie der Moralprobe." *ZRGG* 22 (1970): 164-167.

0637 Maston, T.B. "Ethical Content in Job." *SWJT* 14 (1971): 43-56.

0638 Raurell, Frederic. "Ètica de Job i llibertat de Déu." *Revista Catalana de Teología* 4 (1979): 5-24.

0639 Newsom, C.A. "The Moral Sense of Nature: Ethics in the Light of God's Speech to Job." *PSB* 15 (1994): 9-27.

0640 Oeming, Manfred. "Ethik in der Spätzeit des Alten Testaments am Beispiel von Hiob 31 und Tobit 4." In Peter Mommer and Winfried Thiel (eds.). *Altes Testament Forschung und Wirkung* [festschrift for Henning Graf Reventlow]. Frankfurt am Main: Peter Lang, 1994, pp. 159-173.

Evil

0641 Mattioli, A. "Le ultime ragioni dell'esistenza del male e sella sofferenza in Giobbe." In *La Sapienza della Croce oggi* 3 (1976): 157-187.

0642 Böhles, M. "Von der Macht und Ohnmacht des Bösen." *OrdKor* 18 (1977): 129-146

0643 Nemo, Philippe. *Job et l'excès du mal.* Paris: Grasset, 1978.

0644 Lacocque, André. "Job and the Symbolism of Evil." *BR* 24 (1979): 7-19.

0645 Lafont, G. "L'excès du malheur et la reconnaissance de Diey." *NRT* 101 (1979): 724-739.

0646 Gladson, Jerry. *Who Said Life Is Fair? Job and the Problem of Evil.* Washington: Review and Herald, 1985.

0647 Gibson, J.C.L. "On Evil in the Book of Job." In Lyle Eslinger (ed.). *Ascribe to the Lord: Biblical and Other Studies* [JSOTSup, 67]. Sheffield: Academic Press, 1988, pp. 399-419.

0648 Ravasi, Gianfranco. "Giobbe: male fisico e male morale." *Parola, Spirito e Vita* 19 (1989): 83-94.

0649 Nash, Richard T. "Job's Misconception: A Critical Analysis of the Problem of Evil in the Philosophical Theology of Charles Hartshorne." Dissertation, Leuven, 1991.

0650 Mason, Mike. "The Wizard of Uz: Meditations on Job." *Crux* 27/2 (1991): 35-43.

0651 Good, Edwin M. "The Problem of Evil in the Book of Job." In Leo G. Perdue and W. Clark Gilpin (eds.). *The Voice from the Whirlwind: Interpreting the Book of Job*. Nashville: Abingdon Press, 1992, pp. 50-69.

0652 Vermeylen, J. "Le méchant dans les discours des amis de Job." In W. Beuken (ed.), *The Book of Job* [BETL, 114]. Leuven: University Press, 1994, pp. 101-128.

0653 van der Zee, William R. *Deliver Us from Evil: Is Something Wrong between God and Me?* North Andover: Genesis, 1996.

Faith

0654 Stockhammer, S.E. "Job's Problem." *Judaism* 2 (1953): 247-253.

0655 Gordis, Robert. "The Temptation of Job - Tradition versus Experience." *Judaism* 4 (1955): 195-208

0656 Strolz, W. *Hiobs Auflehnung gegen Gott* [Opuscula aus Glaube und Dichtung, 36]. Pfullingen: Neske, 1967.

0657 Michel, D. "Hiob: Wegen Gott gegen Gott." In *Israels Glaube im Wandel*. Berlin 1968, pp. 252-277.

0658 Schmidt, Paul. "Sinnfrage und Glaubenskrise: Ansätze zu einter kritischen Theologie der Schöpfung im Buche Hiob." *Geist und Leben* 45 (1972): 348-363.

0659 Stockhammer, S.E. "Job's Problem." In Robert Gordis (ed.). *Faith and Reason:* Essays in Judaism. New York 1973, pp. 54-60.

0660 Scammon, J.H. *If I Could Find God: Anguish and Faith in the Book of Job*. Valley Forge (PA): Judson, 1974.

0661 Snell, P. "A Journey of Faith." *TBT* 20 (1982): 334-337.

0662 Carson, D.A. "Mystery and Faith in Job 38:1 - 42:16." In Roy B. Zuck (ed.). *Sitting with Job: Selected Studies on the Book of Job*. Grand Rapids: Baker, 1992, pp. 373-379.

0663 Tomasoni, Francesco. "Giobbe, modello di fede razionale in Kant." *Humanitas* 46 (1991): 267-269.

0664 Fleming, Daniel E. "Job: The Tale of Patient Faith and the Book of God's Dilemma." *VT* 44/4 (1994): 468-482.

0665 Vogels, Walter. "Job's Superficial Faith in His First Reactions to Suffering (Job 1:20-23; 2:8-10). *Eglise et Théologie* 25 (1994): 343-339.

Fear of God

0666 Lacoque, A. "Est-ce gratuitement que Job craint Dieu?" In E. Amado-Valensi, et al. (eds.). *Mélanges André Neher*. Paris 1975, pp. 175-179.

0667 Ararat, Nisan. "Concerning Job's 'Fear of God'." *Beth Mikra* 29 (1983-84): 263-278.

0668 Tilley, Terrence. "Considering Job: Does Job Fear God for Naught?" *The Evils of Theodicy*. Washington, DC: Georgetown University Press, 1991, pp. 89-112.

0669 Wilson, Lindsay. "The Book of Job and the Fear of God." *TynBul* 46 (1995): 59-79.

Genre (form)

0670 Fohrer, Georg. "Form und Funktion in der Hiobdichtung." *ZDMG* 109 (1959): 31-49.

0671 Raphael, D.D. "Tragedy and Religion." In P.S. Sanders (ed.). *Twentieth Century Interpretations of the Book of Job: A Collection of Essays*. Englewood Cliffs: Prentice-Hall, 1968, pp. 46-55.

0672 Terrien, Samuel. "La poème de Job: drama para-rituel du Nouvel-An?" *VTSup* 17 (1969): 220-235.

0673 Kurzweil, B. "Job and the Possibility of Biblical Tragedy." In A.A. Cohen (ed.). *Arguments and Doctrines*. New York 1970, pp. 323-344.

0674 Holland, J.A. "On the Form of the Book of Job." *AJBA* 1 (1972): 160-177.

0675 Urbrock, W.J. "Reconciliation of Opposites in the Dramatic Ordeal of Job." *Semeia* 5 (1976): 147-154.

0676 Alonso Schökel, Luis. "Toward a Dramatic Reading of the Book of Job." In Robert Polzin and David Robertson (eds.). *Studies in the Book of Job* [Semeia, 7]. Missoula: Scholars Pres, 1977, pp. 45-61.

0677 Whedbee, J. William. "The Comedy of Job." In Robert Polzin and David Robertson (eds.). *Studies in the Book of Job* [Semeia, 7]. Missoula: Scholars Pres, 1977, pp. 1-39.

0678 Ahroni, R. "An Examination of the Literary Genre of the Book of Job." *Tarbiz* 49 (1979-80): 1-13.

0679 Urbrock, William J. "Job as Drama: Tragedy or Comedy?" *Currents in Theology and Mission* 8 (1981): 35-40.

0680 Fisch, Harold. "Job: Tragedy Is Not Enough." *Poetry with a Purpose: Biblical Poetics and Interpretation* [Indiana Studies in Biblical Literature]. Bloomington: Indiana University Press, 1988, pp. 26-42.

0681 Erikson, Gösta and Kristina Jonasson. "Jobsbokens juridiska grundmönster." *STK* 65/2 (1989): 64-69.

0682 Alexander, Jon. "Job Considered as a Conversion Account." *Spirituality Today* 42 (1990): 126-139.

0683 Dell, Katherine J. *The Book of Job as Sceptical Literature* [BZAW, 197]. Berlin: Walter de Gruyter, 1991.

0684 Fontaine, Carol R. "Wounded Hero on a Shaman's Quest: Job in the Context of Folk Literature." In Leo G. Perdue and W. Clark Gilpin (eds.). *The Voice from the Whirlwind: Interpreting the Book of Job*. Nashville: Abingdon Press, 1992, pp. 70-85.

0685 Gowan, Donald E. "Reading Job as a 'Wisdom Script'." *JSOT* 55 (1992): 85-96.

0686 Schlobin, Roger C. "Prototypic Horror: The Genre of the Book of Job." In G. Achele and T. Pippin (eds.). *Fantasy and the Bible* [*Semeia* #60]. Atlanta: Scholars Press, 1992, pp. 23-38.

0687 Dailey, Thomas F. "The Book of Job as Optimistic Wisdom." *Journal of Theta Alpha Kappa* 18/1 (1994): 3-16.

0688 Cheney, Michael. *Dust, Wind and Agony: Character, Speech and Genre in Job* [ConBOT, 36]. Stockholm: Almqvist and Wiksell, 1995.

God-Question

0689 Vischer, Wilhelm. "God's Truth and Man's Lie — A Study in the Message of the Book of Job." *Int* 15 (1961): 131-146.

0690 Ciuba, E. "Job and the God Question." *TBT* 54 (1971): 376-385.

0691 Haag, H. *Ijobs Fragen an Gott*. Stuttgart: KBW-Verlag, 1972.

0692 Harris, R. Laird. "The Book of Job and Its Doctrine of God." *Grace Journal* 13 (1972): 3-33.

0693 Alonso Díaz, J. "La experiencia de Job en la órbita del amor de Dios." *Biblia y Fe* 1 (1975): 66-81.

0694 Raurell, Frederic. "Ètica de Job i llibertat de Déu." *Revista Catalana de Teología* 4 (1979): 5-24.

0695 Willi-Plein, Ina. "Hiobs immer aktuelle Frage." In Karl Illman (ed.). *Der Herr ist einer, unser gemeinsames Erbe*. ÅbO 1979, pp. 122-136.

0696 Deselaers, Paul et al. *Sehnsucht nach dem lebendigen Gott: Das Buch Ijob*. Stuttgart: Katholisches Bibelwerk, 1983.

0697 Ravasi, Gianfranco. *Giobbe: il silenzio di Dio*. Roma: Paoline, 1984.

0698 Priest, John. "Job and *J.B.*: The Goodness of God or the Godness of Good." *Horizons* 12/2 (1985): 265-283.

0699 Sia, Santiago. "Reflections on Job's Question." *Spirituality Today* 37 (1985): 234-242.

0700 Mettinger, Tryggve. "Job and His God." *In Search of God: The Meaning and Message of the Everlasting Names.* Philadelphia 1988, pp. 175-200.

0701 Riley, William. "The Book of Job and the Terrible Truth about God." *ScrB* 18 (1988): 322-326.

0702 Pleins, J. David. "'Why Do You Hide Your Face?' - Divine Silence and Speech in the Book of Job." *Int* 48/3 (1994): 229-238.

History of Interpretation - Patristic

0703 Guillaumin, Marie-Louise. "Recherches sur l'exégèse patristique de Job." In E.A. Livingstone (ed.). *Studia Patristica* [12]. Oxford: University, 1975, pp. I, 304-308.

0704 Baskin, J.R. "Job as Moral Exemplar in Ambrose." *Vigiliae Christianae* 35/3 (1981): 222-231.

0705 Doignon, J. "Corpora Vitiorum Materies: Une formule-cle du fragment sur Job d'Hilare de Poitiers inspiré d'Origene et transmis par Augustin (*Contra Iulianum* 2, 8, 27)." *Vigiliae Christianae* 35/3 (1981): 209-221.

0706 Fontaine, Jacques. "Augustin, Grégoire et Isidore: Esquisse d'une recherche sur le style des Moralia in Iob." In Jacques Fontaine, et al. (eds.). *Grégoire le Grand.* Paris: CNRS, 1982, pp. 499-509.

0707 Hagedorn, Ursula and J. Deiter (tr. & ed.). *J. Chrisostomos Kommentar zu Hiob* [Patristische Texte und Studien, 35]. Berlin: de Gruyter, 1990.

0708 Vincent, Monique. "El libro de Job en la predicación de san Augustín." *Augustinus* 36 (1991): 355-360.

0709 Ciccarese, Maria Pia. "Una esegeis 'double face': introduzione alla Expositio in Ijob del presbitero Filippo." *Annali di Storia dell'Esegesi* 9/2 (1992): 483-492.

0710 Hagedorn, U. and D. Hagerdorn (eds.). *Die älteren griechischen Katenen zum Buch Hiob, Bant I: Einleitung, Prolog und Epilog, Fragmente zu Hiob 1,1-8,22* [Patristische Texte und Studien, 40]. Berlin: de Gruyter, 1994.

0711 Reventlow, Henning Graf. "Hiob der Mann. Ein altkirchliches Ideal bei Didymus dem Blinden." In *Text and Theology* [festschrift for Magne Saebø]. Oslo: Verbum 1994, pp. 213-227.

History of Interpretation - Medieval

0712 Besserman, L.L. *The Legend of Job in the Middle Ages.* Cambridge, MA: Harvard, 1979.

0713 Manzanedo, Marcos F. "La antropologia filosófica en el comentario tomista al libro de Job." *Ang* 62 (1985): 419-471.

0714 Ferreiro, Alberto. "Job in the Sermons of Caesarius of Arles." *Recherches de Théologie Ancienne et Medievale* 54 (1987): 13-26.

0715 Schreiner, Susan E. "'Where Shall Wisdom Be Found?' Gregory's Interpretation of Job." *American Benedictine Review* 39 (1988): 321-342.

0716 Damico, Anthony (tr.) and Martin D. Yaffe (ed.). *Thomas Aquinas' Literal Exposition of Job: A Scriptural Commentary Concerning Providence* [AAR Classics, 7]. Atlanta: Scholars Press, 1989.

0717 Coggi, Roberto. "La prova morale dell'immortalità dell'anima nel commento de S. Tommaso al libro de Giobbe." *Divus Thomas* 95,1 (1992): 157-163.

0718 Greenberg, Moshe. "Did Job Really Exist? An Issue of Medieval Exegesis." In M. Fishbane, et al. (eds.). *'Sha'arei Talmon': Studies in the Bible, Qumran, and the Ancient Near East.* Winona Lake: Eisenbrauns, 1992.

0719 Perani, Mauro. "Frammenti ebraici di un commento medievale sconosciuto a Proverbi e Giobbe." *Annali di Storoa dell'Esegesi* 9,2 (1992): 589-608.

0720 Yaffe, Martin D. "Providence in Medieval Aristotelianism: Moses Maimonides and Thomas Aquinas on the Book of Job." In Leo G. Perdue and W. Clark Gilpin (eds.). *The Voice from the Whirlwind: Interpreting the Book of Job*. Nashville: Abingdon Press, 1992, pp. 111-128.

History of Interpretation - Rabbinic

0721 Laks, H. Joel. "The Enigma of Job: Maimonides and the Moderns." *JBL* 83/4 (1964): 345-364.

0722 Hanson, A.T. "Job in Early Christianity and Rabbinic Judaism." *CQ* 2 (1969): 147-151.

0723 Silver, D.J. "Nachmanides' Commentary on the Book of Job." *JQR* 60 (1969): 9-26.

0724 Jacobs, I. "The Book of Job in Rabbinic Thought." Dissertation, London University College, 1970.

0725 Leibowitz, Joseph. *The Image of Job as Reflected in Rabbinic Writings*. Disseratation, California (Berkeley), 1987.

0726 Levinger, Jacob. "Maimonides' Exegesis of the Book of Job." In B. Uffenheimer and H. Reventlow (eds.). *Creative Biblical Exegesis: Christian and Jewish Hermeneutics through the Centuries* [JSOTSup, 59]. Sheffield 1988, pp. 81-88.

0727 Baskin, Judith R. "Rabbinic Interpretations of Job." In Leo G. Perdue and W. Clark Gilpin (eds.). *The Voice from the Whirlwind: Interpreting the Book of Job*. Nashville: Abingdon Press, 1992, pp. 101-110.

0728 Kimhi, Moses. *Commentary on the Book of Job: Edited, with Introduction and Notes* [South Florida Studies in the History of Judaism, 64]. Atlanta: Scholars Press, 1992.

0729 Schreiner, Stefan. "Der gottesfürchtige Rebell." *ZTK* 89/2 (1992): 159-171.

0730 Yaffe, Martin D. "Providence in Medieval Aristotelianism: Moses Maimonides and Thomas Aquinas on the Book of Job." In Leo G. Perdue and W. Clark Gilpin (eds.). *The Voice from the Whirlwind: Interpreting the Book of Job*. Nashville: Abingdon Press, 1992, pp. 111-128.

0731 Weinberg, J. "Job versus Abraham: The Quest for the Perfect God-Fearer in Rabbinic Tradition." In W. Beuken (ed.), *The Book of Job* [BETL, 114]. Leuven: University Press, 1994, pp. 281-296.

0732 Carpentier, Jean-Marie. "L'interrogation de Job sur la toute-puissance de Dieu et la conversion de cette interrogation dans Le Guide des Egarés de Mäimonide." *MScRel* 53 (1996): 39-50.

History of Interpretation - Reformation

0733 Calvin, John. *Sermons from Job*. Selected and translated by L. Nixon. Grand Rapids: Baker, 1979.

0734 Schreiner, Susan. "'Through a Mirror Dimly': Calvin's Sermons on Job." *CJT* 21 (1986): 175-192.

0735 Schreiner, Susan E. "Exegesis and Double Justice in Calvin's Sermons on Job." *CH* 58 (1989): 322-338.

0736 Schreiner, Susan E. "'Why do the wicked live?': Job and David in Calvin's Sermons on Job." In Leo G. Perdue and W. Clark Gilpini (eds.). *The Voice from the Whirlwind: Interpreting the Book of Job*. Nashville: Abingdon Press, 1992, 129-143.

History of Interpretation - Jewish

0737 Carstensen, R.N. "The Persistence of the 'Elihu' Tradition in Later Jewish Writers." *Lexington Theological Quarterly* 2/2 (1967): 37-46.

0738 Goldschmidt, H.L. "Hiob im neuzeitlichen Judentum." *Weltgespräch* 2 (1967): 41-55.

0739 Susman, M. *Das Buch Hiob und das Schicksal des jüdischen Volkes*. Freiburg: Herder, 1968.

0740 Glatzer, Norman N. "Jüdische Ijob-Deutungen in den ersten Christlichen Jahrunderten." *Freiburger Rundbrief* 26 (1974): 31-34.

0741 Curtis, John Briggs. "Some Jewish Interpretations of Job 37:6 — Midrash or Ancient Cosmogony?" *PEGLMBS* 9 (1989): 113-123.

0742 Ehrlich, E.L. "Hiob in der jüdischen Tradition." In *Festschrift for H. Vorgrimler*, 1994, pp. 38-55 (#83)

History of Interpretation - Christian

0743 Leloir, L. "Job: Christian and Monastic Perspectives." *Monastic Studies* 6 (1968): 51-71.

0744 Hanson, A.T. "Job in Early Christianity and Rabbinic Judaism." *CQ* 2 (1969): 147-151.

0745 Schulweis, Harold M. "Karl Barth's Job: Morality and Theodicy." *JQR* 65/3 (1975): 156-167.

History of Interpretation - Modern

0746 Laks, H. Joel. "The Enigma of Job: Maimonides and the Moderns." *JBL* 83/4 (1964): 345-364.

0747 Matthews, M.S. "Issues and Answers in the Book of Job and Joban Issues in Three Twentieth Century Writers: C. Jung, R. Frost, and J.B. MacLeish." Dissertation, Florida State University, 1976.

0748 Vogler, Thomas A. "Eighteenth-Century Logology and the Book of Job." *Religion and Literature* 20/3 (1988): 25-47.

0749 Lamb, Jonathan. *The Rhetoric of Suffering: Reading the Book of Job in the Eighteenth Century.* Cambridge: Oxford University Pres, 1995.

0749a Bechtel, Lyn M. "A Feminist Approach to the Book of Job." In Athalya Brenner (ed.). *A Feminist Companion to Wisdom Literature* [The Feminist Companion to the Bible, 9]. Sheffield: Academic Press, 1995, pp. 186-200.

Holiness

0750 Kaufmann, U.M. "Expostulation with the Divine: A Note on Contrasting ·Attitudes in Greek and Hebrew Piety." In P.S. Sanders (ed.). *Twentieth Century Interpretations of the Book of Job: A Collection of Essays.* Englewood Cliffs: Prentice-Hall, 1968, pp. 66-77.

0751 Leloir, L. "Lectio divina: Job 1,1-5 sainteté juive et sainteté chrètienne." *Collectanea Cisterciensia* 32 (1970): 268-288.

0752 Schreiner, Stefan. "Der gottesfürchtige Rebell." *ZTK* 89/2 (1992): 159-171.

Hope

0753 Lévêque, Jean. "Job, ou l'espoir déraciné." *VSpir* 125 (1971): 287-304.

0754 Brates (Cavero), L. "La esperanza en el libro de Job." In *XXX Sem B Esp* (Madrid) 1970, pp. 21-34.

0755 Riebl, M. *In Krise und Hoffnung: ein Arbeitsheft zum Buch Ijob* [Gespräche zur Bibell, 12]. Klosterneuburg: ÖsterrKB, 1981.

Iconography

0756 Marqusee, Michael. *The Book of Job, illustrated by William Blake* [Masterpieces of the Illustrated Book]. New York: Paddington, 1976.

0757 Raine, Kathleen Jessie. "The Human Face of God: William Blake and the Book of Job." *Commonweal* 110 (Feb 1983) 91.

0758 Durand, Jannic. "Note sure une iconographie méconnue: le 'saint roi Job'." *Cahiers Archéologiques* 32 (1984): 113-135.

0759 Perraymond, Myla. "Giobbe nell'iconografia sepolcrale e nalle primitiva letterature cristiana." Dissertation, Istituto Archaeologico Christiana. Rome 1986.

0760 Cornelius, Izak. "The Sun Epiphany in Job 38:12-15 and the Iconography of the Gods in the Ancient Near East - The Palestinian Connection." *JNSL* 16 (1990): 25-43.

0760a Gitay, Zefira. "The Portrayal of Job's Wife and Her Representation in the Visual Arts." In Astrid B. Beck, et al. (eds.). *Fortunate the Eyes That See* [festschrift for D.N. Freedman]. Grand Rapids: Eerdmans, 1995, pp. 516-526.

0761 Terrien, Samuel. *The Iconography of Job through the Centuries: Artists as Biblical Interpreters*. Pennsylvania State University, 1995.

Intertextuality

0762 Fishbane, Michael. "The Book of Job and Inner Biblical Discourse." In Leo G. Perdue and W. Clark Gilpin (eds.). *The Voice from the Whirlwind: Interpreting the Book of Job*. Nashville: Abingdon Press, 1992, pp. 86-98.

0763 Mettinger, Tryggve N.D. "Intertextuality: Allusion and Vertical Context Systems in Some Job Passages." In Heather A. McKay and David J.A. Clines (eds.). *Of Prophets' Visions and the Wisdom of Sages* [festschrift for R. Norman Whybray; JSOTSup, 163]. Sheffield: Almond Press, 1993, pp. 257-280.

0764 Marnewick, J.C. and A.P.B. Breytenbach. "Die boek Job gelees vanuit 'n Ou-Testamentiese verbondsperspektief." *HerTS* 50/4 (1994): 923-935.

Intertextuality - Torah

0765 Frye, J.B. "The Use of Pentateuchal Traditions in the Book of Job." In W.C. van Wyk (ed.). *Old Testament Essays: Studies in the Pentateuch.* Pretoria: University Department of Semitic Languages, 1977, pp. 13-20.

0766 Christensen, D. "Job and the Age of the Patriarchs in the Old Testament." *Perspectives in Religious Studies* 13 (1986): 225-228.

0767 Meier, Sam. "Job i-ii: A Reflection of Genesis i-iii." *VT* 39 (1989): 183-193.

0768 Klein, Joseph P. "How Job Fulfills God's Word to Cain." *BRev* 9/3 (1993): 40-43.

Intertextuality - Historical

0769 Hoffman, Rudolf. "Eine Parallele zur Rahmenerzählung des Buches Hiob in I Chr 7, 20-29?" *ZAW* 92 (1980): 120-132.

0770 Joosten, J. "La macrostructure du livre de Job et quelques parallèles (Jérémie 45; 1 Rois 19)." In W. Beuken (ed.), *The Book of Job* [BETL, 114]. Leuven: University Press, 1994, pp. 400-404.

0771 Oeming, Manfred. "Ethik in der Spätzeit des Alten Testaments am Beispiel von Hiob 31 und Tobit 4." In Peter Mommer and Winfried Thiel (eds.). *Altes Testament Forschung und Wirkung* [festschrift for Henning Graf Reventlow]. Frankfurt am Main: Peter Lang, 1994, pp. 159-173.

Intertextuality - Prophets

0772 Bardtke, H. "Prophetische Züge im Buch Hiob." In F. Maass (ed.). *Das Ferne und nahe Wort* [festschrift L. Rost; BZAW, 105]. Berlin: A. Töpelmann, 1967, pp. 1-10.

0773 Curtis, John Briggs. "Elihu and Deutero-Isaiah: A Study in Literary Dependence." *PEGLMBS* 10 (1990): 31-38.

0774 Janzen, J.G. "On the Moral Nature of God's Power: Yahweh and the Sea in Job and Deutero-Isaiah." *CBQ* 56 (1994): 458-478.

0775 Joosten, J. "La macrostructure du livre de Job et quelques parallèles (Jérémie 45; 1 Rois 19)." In W. Beuken (ed.), *The Book of Job* [BETL, 114]. Leuven: University Press, 1994, pp. 400-404.

Intertextuality - Writings

0776 Benamozegh, E. "L'immortalità dell'anima in Giobbe e nei Proverbi." *Annali di Storia Ebraica* 8 (1977): 145-172.

Justice

0777 Laserson, Max. "Power and Justice: Hobbes versus Job." *Judaism* 2 (1953): 52-60.

0778 Cepeda Calzada, P. "El problema de la justicia en Job." *Crisis* 20 (1973): 243-290.

0779 Cepeda Calzada, P. *El problema de la justicia en Job.* Madrid: Prensa Española, 1975.

0780 Hubermann-Scholnick, S. "Lawsuit in the Book of Job." Dissertation, Brandeis University, 1976.

0781 Loader, J.A. "Different Reactions of Job and Qoheleth to the Doctrine of Retribution." In W. Wyk (ed.). *Studies in Wisdom Literature* [Ou-Testamentiese Werkgemeenskap In Suider-Afrika, 15]. Hercules, SA: NHW Press, 1981, pp. 43-48.

0782 Ruprecht, E. "Leiden und Gerechtigkeit bei Hiob." *ZTK* 73 (1976): 424-445.

0783 Halpern, B. "Yahweh's Summary Justice in Job." *VT* 28 (1978): 472-474.

0784 Gerber, I.J. *Job on Trial: A Book for Our Times.* Gastonia (NC) 1982.

0785 Huberman-Scholnick, Sylvia. "The Meaning of *mišpat* in the Book of Job." *JBL* 101 (1982): 521-529.

0785a Holm-Nielsen, Svend. "Die Verteidigung für die Gerechtigkeit Gottes." *Scandinavian Journal of the Old Testament* 2 (1987): 69-89.

0786 Heckelman, Joseph. "The Liberation of Job." *Dor le Dor* 17/1 (1988-89): 128-132.

0787 Lasine, Stuart. "Bird's-Eye and Worm's-Eye Views of Justice in the Book of Job." *JSOT* 42 (1988): 29-53.

0788 Gilkey, Langdon. "Power, Order, Justice, and Redemption: Theological Comments on Job." In Leo G. Perdue and W. Clark Gilpin (eds.). *The Voice from the Whirlwind: Interpreting the Book of Job*. Nashville: Abingdon Press, 1992, pp. 159-171.

0789 Bakon, Shimon. "God and Man on Trial." *JBQ* 21 (1993): 226-235.

Language

0790 Dobson, J.H. "Translating Job — Prose or Poetry?" *BT* 23 (1972): 243-244.

0791 Frye, J.B. "Legal Language in the Book of Job." Dissertation, King's College (London), 1972-73.

0792 Urbrock, W.J. "Formula and Theme in the Song-Cycle of Job." *SBL Proceedings* 108/2 (1972): 459-487.

0793 Snaith, N.H. "The Introductions to the Speeches in the Book of Job. Are They in Prose or in Verse?" *Textus* 8 (1973): 133-137.

0794 Dahood, Mitchell J. "Chiasmus in Job: A Text-Critical and Philological Criterion." In Howard N. Bream, Ralph D. Heim, and Carey A. Moore (eds). *A Light to My Path*. Philadelphia: Temple University, 1974, pp. 119-130.

0795 Weimer, J.D. "Job's Complaint: A Study of Its Limits and Form, Content and Significance." Dissertation, Union Theological Seminary, 1974.

0796 Urbrock, W.J. "Oral Antecedents to Job: A Survey of Formulas and Formulaic Systems." *Semeia* 5 (1976): 111-137.

0797 Frye, J.B. "The Use of *māšāl* in the Book of Job." *Semitics* 5 (1977): 59-66.

0798 van Selms, A. "Motivated Interrogative Sentences in the Book of Job." *Semitics* 6 (1978): 28-35.

0799 Fohrer, Georg. "Dialog und Kommunikation im Buche Hiob." In M. Gilbert (ed.). *La Sagesse de l'Ancien Testament* [BETL, 51]. Leuven: University Press, 1979, pp. 219-230.

0800 Lipiński, E. "Notes lexicographiques et stylistiques sur le livre de Job." *Folia Orientalia* 21 (1980): 65-82.

0801 Perani, Mauro. "Rilievi sulla terminologia temporale nel libro di Giobbe." *Henoch* 5 (1983): 1-28.

0802 Smick, Elmer B. "Semiological Interpretation of the Book of Job." *WTJ* 46 (1986): 135-149.

0803 Dion, Paul E. "Formulaic Language in the Book of Job: International Background and Ironical Distortions." *SR* 16 (1987): 187-193.

0804 Burden, J.J. "Decision by Debate: Examples of Popular Proverb Performance in the Book of Job." *OTE* 4/1 (1991): 37-65.

0805 van Rensburg, J.F.J. "Wise Men Saying Things by Asking Questions: The Function of the Interrogative in Job 3-14." *OTE* 4/2 (1991): 227-247.

0806 Gosling, Frank. "The Syntax of Hebrew Poetry: An Examination of the Use of Tenses in Poetry, with reference to Job 3/1-42/6." Dissertation, St. Andrew's, 1992.

0807 Moore, Michael S. "Job's Texts of Terror." *CBQ* 55/4 (1993): 662-675.

0808 Vall, Gregory. "From Womb to Tomb: Poetic Imagery and the Book of Job." Dissertation, Catholic University of America, 1993.

0808a Steinmann, Andrew E. "The Graded Numerical Saying in Job." In Astrid B. Beck, et al. (eds.). *Fortunate the Eyes That See* [festschrift for D.N. Freedman]. Grand Rapids: Eerdmans, 1995, pp. 288-297.

0809 Cheney, Michael. *Dust, Wind and Agony: Character, Speech and Genre in Job* [ConBOT, 36]. Stockholm: Almqvist and Wiksell, 1995.

0810 Noegel, Scott B. *Janus Parallelism in the Book of Job*. Sheffield: Academic Press, 1996.

0811 Noegel, Scott B. "Janus Parallelism in Job and Its Literary Significance." *JBL* 115/2 (1996): 313-320.

0811a Sarna, N.M. "Notes on the Use of the Definite Article in the Poetry of Job." In M. Fox, et al. (eds.). *Texts, Temples, and Traditions* [festschrift for M. Haran]. Winona Lake: Eisenbrauns, 1996, pp. 279-284.

Literary

0812 Fohrer, Georg. "Zur Vorgeschichte und Komposition des Buches Hiob." *VT* 6 (1956): 249-267.

0813 Berry, D.L. "Scripture and Imaginative Literature: Focus on Job." *Journal of General Education* 19 (1967): 119-131.

0814 Gray, G.B. "The Purpose and Method of the Writer." In P.S. Sanders (ed.). *Twentieth Century Interpretations of the Book of Job: A Collection of Essays*. Englewood Cliffs: Prentice-Hall, 1968, pp. 36-45.

0815 Maillot, A. "Job, livre païen." *Foi et Vie* 69/5 (1970): 2-15.

0816 Stockton, E. "Literary Development of the Book of Job." *Australian Catholic Record* 49 (1972): 137-143.

0817 Good, Edwin M. "Job and the Literary Task: a response." *Soundings* 56 (1973): 470-484.

0818 Miles, John A. "Gagging on Job, or The Comedy of Religious Exhaustion." In Robert Polzin and David Robertson (eds.). *Studies in the Book of Job* [Semeia, 7]. Missoula: Scholars Press, 1977, pp. 71-126.

0819 Baker, J.A. "The Book of Job: Unity and Meaning." In E. Livingston (ed.). *Studia Biblica, I* [6th International Congress on Biblical Studies; JSOTSup, 11]. Sheffield: University, 1979, pp. 17-26.

0820 Lichtenstein, Aaron. "Toward a Literary Understanding of the Book of Job." *Hebrew Studies* 20/21 (1979-80): 34-35.

0821 Sawyer, J.F.A. "The Authorship and Structure of the Book of Job." In E. Livinstone (ed.). *Studia Biblica, I* [6th International Congress on Biblical Studies]. Sheffield: University, 1979, pp. 253-257.

0822 Lévêque, Jean. "La datation du livre de Job." In J. Emerton (ed.). *Congress Volume* [VTSup, 32]. Leiden: Brill, 1981, pp. 206-219.

0823 Weimar, Peter. "Literarkritisches zur Ijobnovelle." *BN* 12 (1980): 62-80.

0824 Parsons, Gregory W. "Literary Features of the Book of Job." *BSac* 138 (1981): 213-229.

0825 Greenberg, Moshe. "Job." In R. Alter and F. Kermode (eds.). *The Literary Guide to the Bible*. Cambridge, MA: Harvard University Press, 1987, pp. 283-304.

0826 Radzinowicz, Mary Ann. "How and Why the Literary Establishment Caught Up with the Bible: Instancing the Book of Job." *Christianity and Literature* 39/1 (1989): 77-89.

0827 Lerner, Berel Dov. "Faith, Fiction, and the Jewish Scriptures." *Judaism* 39/2 (1990)0 215-220.

0828 Penchansky, David. *The Betrayal of God: Ideological Conflict in Job* [Literary Currents in Biblical Interpretation]. Louisville: Westminster/John Knox Press, 1990.

0829 Caesar, Lael O. "Character in Job." Dissertation, Wisconsin University, 1991.

0830 Dailey, Thomas F. "The Aesthetics of Repentance: Re-Reading the Phenomenon of Job." *BTB* 23 (1993): 64-70.

0831 Cheney, Michael. *Dust, Wind and Agony: Character, Speech and Genre in Job* [ConBOT, 36]. Stockholm: Almqvist and Wiksell, 1994.

0832 Fisch, H. "Being Possessed by Job." *Literature and Theology* 8 (1994): 280-295.

0833 Langenhorst, G. *Hiob unser Zeitgenosse: Die literarische Hiob-Rezeption im 20. Jahrhundert als theologische Herausforderung* [Theologie und Literatur, 1]. Mains: Matthias-Grünewald, 1994.

0834 van Wolde, Ellen. "A Text-Semantic Study of the Hebrew Bible, Illustrated with Noah and Job." *JBL* 113/1 (1994): 19-35.

0835 Clines, David J.A. "Deconstructing the Book of Job." *Bible Review* 11/2 (1995): 30-35, 43-44.

Motifs

0836 Aiura, T. "Wisdom Motifs in the Joban Poem." *Kwansei Gakuin University Annual Studies* 15 (1966): 1-20.

0837 Bergant, Dianne. "An Historico-Critical Study of the Anthropological Traditions and Motifs in Job." Dissertation, St. Louis University, 1975.

0838 Forrest, R.W.E. "The Creation Motif in the Book of Job." Dissertation, MacMaster University, 1975.

0839 Parsons, Gregory W. "Literary Features of the Book of Job." *BSac* 138 (1981): 213-229.

0840 Smick, Elmer B. "Architectonics, Structural Poems, and Rhetorical Devices in the Book of Job." In W. Kaiser and R. Youngblood (eds.). *A Tribute to Gleason Archer*. Chicago 1986, pp. 87-104.

0841 Burden, J.J. "Decision by Debate: Examples of Popular Proverb Performance in the Book of Job." *OTE* 4 (1991): 37-65.

0842 Vall, Gregory. "From Womb to Tomb: Poetic Imagery and the Book of Job." Dissertation, Catholic University of America, 1993.

0843 Borgonovo, Gianantonio. *La notte e il suo sole: luce et tenebre nel Libro di Giobbe: analisi simbolica* [AnBib, 135]. Rome: Pontifical Biblical Institute, 1995.

Motifs - irony/parody

0844 Hoffman, Yair. "Irony in the Book of Job." *Immanuel* 17 (1983-84): 7-21.

0845 Brinker, M. "On the Ironic Use of Job." In D.H. Hirsch (ed.). *Biblical Patterns in Modern Literature* [BJS, 87]. Chico, CA: Scholars, 1984, pp. 115-126.

0846 Lichtenstein, Aaron. "Irony in the Book of Job." *Dor le Dor* 13 (1984): 41-42.

0847 Sarrazin, Bernard. "Du rire dans la Bible? La théophanie de Job comme parodie." *RevScRel* 76 (1988): 39-56.

Motifs - law

0848 Many, G. "Der Rechtsstreit mit Gott im Hiobbuch." Dissertation, München, 1970.

0849 Roberts, J.J.M. "Job's Summons to Yahweh: The Exploitation of a Legal Metaphor." *ResQ* 16 (1973): 159-165.

0850 Holbert, J.C. "The Function and Significance of the Klage in the Book of Job, with Special Reference to the Incidence of Formal and Verbal Irony." Dissertation, Southern Methodist University, 1975.

0851 Harrison, George. "Legal Terms in Job." *Bible Illustrator* 13 (1987): 13-15.

0852 Hartley, J.E. "From Lament to Oath: A Study of Progression in the Speeches of Job." In W. Beuken (ed.), *The Book of Job* [BETL, 114]. Leuven: University Press, 1994, pp. 79-100.

Motifs - metaphor

0853 Perdue, Leo G. *Wisdom in Revolt: Metaphorical Theology in the Book of Job* [JSOTSup, 112]. Sheffield: Almond Press, 1991.

0854 Dailey, Thomas F. *The Repentant Job: A Ricoeurian Icon for Biblical Theology.* Lanham, MD: University Press of America, 1994.

Motifs - mythology

0855 Toynbee, A.J. "Challenge and Response: The Mythological Clue." In P.S. Sanders (ed.). *Twentiety Century Interpretations of the Book of Job: A Collection of Essays.* Englewood Cliffs: Prentice-Hall, 1968, pp. 86-97.

0856 Michel, W.L. "The Ugaritic Texts and the Mythological Expressions in the Book of Job (Including a New Translation and Philological Notes on the Book of Job)." Dissertation, University of Wisconsin, 1970.

0857 Smick, Elmer B. "Mythology and the Book of Job." *JETS* 13 (1970): 101-108.

0858 von Orelli, A. "Hiob: Deutung eines biblischen Mythos." *Reformatio* 25 (1976): 74-82, 148-158.

0859 Smick, Elmer B. "Another Look at the Mythological Elements in the Book of Job." *WTJ* 40 (1978): 213-228.

0860 Fuchs, Gisela. *Mythos und Hiobdichtung: Aufnahme und Umdeutung altorientalischer Vorstellungen.* Stuttgart: Kohlhammer, 1993.

Narrativity

0861 Cooper, Alan. "Narrative Theory and the Book of Job." *SR* 11 (1982): 35-44.

0862 Habel, Norman. "The Narrative Art of Job: Applying the Principles of Robert Alter." *JSOT* 27 (1983): 101-111.

0863 Lerner, Berel Dov. "Faith, Fiction, and the Jewish Scriptures." *Judaism* 39/2 (1990): 215-220.

New Testament References

0864 Michael, J.H. "Paul and Job: A Neglected Analogy." *ExpTim* 36 (1924-25): 67-70.

0865 Morgan, G. Campbell. *The Answers of Jesus to Job.* Grand Rapids: Baker, 1935.

0866 Schaller, Berndt. "Zum Textcharakter der Hiobzitate im Paulinischen Schrifttum." *ZNW* 71 (1980): 21-26.

0867 Geyer, Carl-Friedrich. "Das Hiobbuch im christlichen und nachchristlichen Kontext: Anmerkungen zur Rezeptionsgeschichte." *Kairos* 28 (1986): 174-195.

0868 Gorringe, Timothy J. "Job and the Pharisees." *Int* 40 (1986): 17-28.

0869 Maia, Pedro A. "Paixão de Jó e paixão de Cristo." *RCB* 10/39 (1986): 132-148.

0870 Hay, David M. "Job and the Problem of Doubt in Paul." In John Carroll, Charles Cosgrove, and Elizabeth Johnson (eds.). *Faith and History* [festschrift for Paul Meyer]. Atlanta: Scholars Press, 1990, pp. 208-222.

0871 Seitz, Christopher. "The Patience of Job in the Epistle of James." In Rüdiger Bartelmus, Thomas Krüger and Helmut Utzschneider (eds). *Konsequente Traditionsgeschichte* [festschrift for Klaus Baltzer; OBO, 126]. Göttingen: Vandenhoeck & Ruprecht, 1993, pp. 373-382.

0872 Baird, Robert M. "On Bad Luck: Job and Jesus." *Journal of Religion and Health* 33 (Winter 1994): 305-312.

0872a Tai, Nicholas H.F. and Peter K.H. Lee. "A Dialogue: Job, Paul, and the Chinese Sages on Suffering." *Theology and Life* 17-19 (1996): 179-195.

Pastoral Concerns

0873 Hulme, William E. *Dialogue in Despair: Pastoral Commentary on the Book of Job.* Nashville: Abingdon, 1968.

0874 Ceresko, Anthony. "The Option for the Poor in the Book of Job." *Indian Theological Studies* 26 (1989): 105-121.

0875 Gibson, John C.L. "The Book of Job and the Care of Souls." *SJT* 42 (1989): 303-317.

0876 Hulme, William. "Pastoral Counseling in the Book of Job." *CJ* 15 (1989): 121-138.

0877 Baruani, Bernard. "Beyond Chapter and Verse: Job — the AIDS Victim." *SIDIC: Service International de Documentation Judo-Chretienne* 23 (1990): 9-11.

0878 Simundson, Daniel J. "Job and His Ministers." In Arland J. Hultgren, et al. (eds.). *All Things New* [festschrift for Roy A. Harrisville; Word and World Supplement Series, 1]. St. Paul: Word and World, 1992, pp. 33-42.

0879 Nimmo, Peter W. "Sin, Evil, and Job: Monotheism as a Psychological and Pastoral Problem." *Pastoral Psychology* 42 (July 1994): 427-439.

0880 Wittenberg, Gunther. "Counselling AIDS Patients: Job as a Paradigm." *Journal of Theology for Southern Africa* 88 (1994): 61-68.

Pastoral Concerns - Preaching

0881 Davis, M. Vernon. "Preaching from Job." *SWJT* 14/1 (1971): 65-76.

0882 Murphy, Roland E. *The Psalms, Job* [OT Witness for Preaching]. Philadelphia 1977.

0883 Habel, Norman C. *Job* [Knox Preaching Guides]. Atlanta: Knox, 1981.

0884 Becker, Edwin L. "Homily on the Book of Job." *Encounter* 49 (1988): 225-228.

0885 Schlafer, David J. "The Book of Job and the Tao Te Ching as antidotes to 'preachy' preaching." *ATR* 74 (1992): 370-375.

0886 Parsons, Greg W. "Guidelines for Understanding and Proclaiming the Book of Job." *BSac* 151 (1994): 393-413.

Pastoral Concerns - Teaching

0887 Bennett, T. Miles. "When a Righteous Man Suffers: A Teaching Outline of the Book of Job." *SWJT* 14/1 (1971): 57-64.

0888 Francisco, C.T. "A Teaching Outline of the Book of Job." *RevExp* 68/4 (1971): 511-520.

0889 Penzenstadler, Joan. "Teaching the Book of Job with a View toward Human Wholeness." *Religious Education* 89 (Spring 1994): 223-231.

Philology

0890 Driver, G.R. "Problems in Job." *AJSL* 53 (1935-36): 160-170.

0891 Sarna, N.M. "Some Instances of the Enclitic -*m* in Job." *JJS* 6 (1955): 108-110.

0892 Driver, G.R. "Problems in the Hebrew Text of Job." *VTSup* 3 (1955): 72-93.

0893 Dahood, Mitchell. "The Root '*ZB* II in Job." *JBL* 78 (1959): 303-309.

0894 Freedman, David Noel. "Orthographic Particularities in the Book of Job." *Ersetz-Israel* 9 (1969): 35-44.

0895 Kusenberg, H. "Das Buch Hiob. Stickworte bei meiner Lektüre." *Merkur* 23 (1969): 543-546.

0896 Barr, James. "Philology and Exegesis: Some General Remarks with Illustrations from Job." In *Questions disputées de l'Ancien Testament: Méthode et théologie* [BETL 33]. Louvain: Leuven University Press, 1974, pp. 39-61.

0897 Boadt, Lawrence. "A Re-Examination of the Third-Yodh Suffix in Job." *UF* 7 (1975): 59-72.

0898 Grabbe, Lester L. *Comparative Philology and the Text of Job: A Study in Methodology* [SBLDS, 34]. Missoula: Scholars Press, 1977.

0899 Lipinksi, Edward. "Notes lexicographiques et stylistiques sur le libre de Job." *Folia Orientalia* 21 (1980): 65-82.

0900 Barr, James. "Hebrew Orthography and the Book of Job." *JSS* 30 (1985): 1-33.

Philology - Northwest Semitic

0901 Dahood, Mitchell. "Northwest Semitic Philology and Job." In J.L. McKenzie (ed.). *The Bible in Current Catholic Thought* [St. Mary's Theology Studies, 1]. New York: Herder and Herder, 1962, pp. 55-74.

0902 Blommerde, Anton. *Northwest Semitic Grammar and Job* [BibOr, 22]. Roma: PIB, 1969.

0903 Ceresko, Anthony. "The A:B::B:A Word Patttern in Hebrew and Northwest Semitic with Special Reference to the Book of Job." *UF* 7 (1976): 73-88.

0904 Michel, W.L. *Job in the Light of Northwest Semitic*, vol I: Prologue and First Cycle of Speeches (Job 1:1 — 14:22) [BibOr, 42]. Roma: PIB, 1987.

Philology - Ugaritic

0905 Feinberg, Charles L. "The Poetic Structure of the Book of Job and Ugaritic Literature." *BSac* 103 (1946): 283-292.

0906 Michel, W.L. "The Ugaritic Texts and the Mythological Expressions in the Book of Job (Including a New Translation and Philological Notes on the Book of Job)." Dissertation, University of Wisconsin, 1970.

0907 Dahood, Mitchell. "Some Rare Parallel Word Pairs in Job and Ugaritic." In R.J. Clifford (ed.). *Festschrift for F.L. Monarty*. Cambridge (MA) 1973, pp. 19-34.

0908 Craigie, Peter C. "Job and Ugaritic Studies." In W. Aufrecht (ed.). *Studies in the Book of Job* [SR Sup, 16]. Waterloo, Ont: W. Laurier University, 1985, pp. 28-35.

0909 Handy, Lowell K. "The Authorization of Divine Power and the Guilt of God in the Book of Job: Useful Ugaritic Parallels." *JSOT* 60 (1993): 107-118.

0910 de Morr, J.C. "Ugarit and the Origin of Job." In G.J. Brooke, et. al (eds.). *Ugarit and the Bible*, pp. 125-257.

Philosophy

0911 Laserson, Max. "Power and Justice: Hobbes versus Job." *Judaism* 2 (1953): 52-60.

0912 Priest, J.F. "Humanism, Scepticism, and Pessimism in Israel." *JAAR* 36 (1968): 311-326.

0913 Gibson, J.C.L. "Eliphaz the Temanite: Portrait of a Hebrew Philosopher." *BETL* 33 (1974): 11-37.

0914 Cox, Dermot. *The Triumph of Impotence: Job and the Tradition of the Absurd* [AnGreg, 212]. Roma: Pontifical Gregorian University, 1978.

0915 Lacocque, André. "Job and the Symbolism of Evil." *BR* 24 (1979): 7-19.

0916 Dornisch, Loretta. "The Book of Job and Ricoeur's Hermeneutics." *Semeia* 19 (1981): 3-22.

0917 Lacoque, André. "Job or the Impotence of Religion and Philosophy." *Semeia* 19 (1981): 33-52.

0918 Loades, A.L. *Kant and Job's Comforters.* Avero 1985.

0919 Manzanedo, Marcos F. "La antropologia filosófica en el comentario tomista al libro de Job." *Ang* 62 (1985): 419-471.

0920 Feuer, Lewis S. "The Book of Job: The Wisdom of Hebrew Stoicism." In R. Joseph Hoffman (ed.). *Biblical versus Secular Ethics: The Conflict.* Buffalo: Prometheus, 1988, pp. 79-97.

0921 Tortolone, Gian Michele. "L'enigma di Giobbe. Destino dell'uomo e silenzio di Dio." *Asprenas* 36 (1989): 22-38.

0922 Wilcox, John T. *The Bitterness of Job: A Philosophical Reading.* Ann Arbor: University of Michigan Press, 1989.

0923 Edwards, Cliff. "Trespassing a Monument: A Lacanian Visit to Uz." *RevExp* 85/2 (1990): 279-294.

0924 Moretto, G. *Giustificazione e interrogazione: Giobbe nella filosofia* [Filosofia e sapere storico]. Napoli: Guida, 1991.

0925 Ronen, Miriam. "The Hebrew Apologia: Job in the Light of Socrates." Dissertation, New York University, 1991.

0926 Tomasoni, Francesco. "Giobbe, modello di fede razionale in Kant." *Humanitas* 46 (1991): 267-269.

0927 Mooney, Edward F. "Kierkegaard's Job Discourse: Getting Back the World." *International Journal for Philosophy of Religion* 34/3 (1993): 151-169.

0928 Williams, James G. "On Job and Writing: Derrida, Girard, and the Remedy-Poison." *SJT* 7 (1993): 32-50.

0929 Astell, Ann W. "Job, Boethius, and Epic Truth." Dissertation, Cornell University, 1994.

0930 Dailey, Thomas. *The Repentant Job: A Ricoeurian Icon for Biblical Theology*. Lanham (MD): University Press of America, 1994.

0931 Borgonovo, Gianantonio. *La notte e il suo sole: luce et tenebre nel Libro di Giobbe: analisi simbolica* [AnBib, 135]. Rome: Biblical Institute, 1995.

Politics

0932 Safire, William. *The First Dissident: The Book of Job in Today's Politics*. New York: Random House, 1992.

0933 Newsom, Carol A. "Cultural Politics and the Reading of Job." *Biblical Interpretation* 1 (1993): 119-138.

Prayer

0934 Patrick, Dale. *Arguing with God: The Angry Prayers of Job*. St. Louis: Bethany Press, 1977.

0935 Patrick, Dale. "Job's Address of God." *ZAW* 91 (1979): 268-282.

0936 Bergant, Dianne. "Things Too Wonderful for Me (Job 42:3)." In Carolyn Osiek and Donald Senior (eds.). *Scripture and Prayer* [festschrift for Carroll Stuhlmueller]. Wilmington: Michael Glazier, 1988, pp. 62-75.

Psychology

0937 Wildberger, H. "Das Hiobproblem und seine neueste Deutung." *Reformatio* 3 (1954): 355-363, 438-448.

0938 Taylor, William S. "Theology and Therapy in Job." *TToday* 12 (1956): 451-462.

0939 Katz, Robert L. "A Psychoanalytic Comment on Job 3:25." *HUCA* 29 (1958): 377-383.

0940 Hedinger, U. "Reflexionen zu C. Jungs Hiobinterpretation." *TZ* 23 (1969): 340-352.

0941 Reid, S.A. "The Book of Job." *Psychoanalytic Review* 60 (1973): 373-391.

0942 Kahn, J.H. *Job's Illness: Loss, Grief and Integration. A Psychological Interpretation.* New York: Pergamon, 1975.

0943 Reynierse, James H. "Behavior Therapy and Job's Recovery." *Journal of Psychology and Theology* 3 (1975): 187-194.

0944 Reynierse, James H. "A Behavioristic Analysis of the Book of Job." *Journal of Psychology and Theology* 3 (1975): 75-81.

0945 Kapusta, M.A. "The Book of Job and the Modern View of Depression." *Annual of Internal Medicine* 86 (1977): 667-672.

0946 Jung, C.G. *Answer to Job.* London: Routledge, 19779.

0947 Vogels, Walter. "The Spiritual Growth of Job: A Psychological Approach to the Book of Job." *BTB* 11 (July 1981): 77-80.

0948 Vogels, Walter. "The Inner Development of Job: One More Look at Psychology and the Book of Job." *ScEs* 35 (1983): 227-230.

0949 Gerritsen, Arthur. "Bibliodrama about Job: Some Preliminary Notes." In *Current Issues in the Psychology of Religion* [eds. J.A. van Belzen and J.M. van der Lans]. Amsterdam: Rodopi, 1986, pp. 112-123.

0950 O'Connor, Daniel J. "The Comforting of Job." *ITQ* 53 (1987): 245-257.

0951 Schimmel, Solomon. "Job and the Psychology of Suffering and Doubt." *Journal of Psychology and Judaism* 11 (1987): 239-249.

0952 Siwy, James M. and Carole E. Smith. "Christian Group Therapy: Sitting with Job." *Journal of Psychology and Theology* 16/4 (1988): 318-323.

0953 van Praag, Herman. "Job's Agony: A Biblical Evocation of Bereavement and Grief." *Judaism* 37 (1988): 175-187.

0954 Maas, Jeannete. "A Psychological Assessment of Job." *Pacific Journal of Theology* 1/2 (1989): 55-68.

0955 Kisch, Jeremy. "Job's Friends: Psychotherapeutic Precursors in the Ancient Near East." *Psychotherapy* 27/1 (1990): 46-52

0956 Achenbaum, W. Andrew and Lucinda Orwoll. "Becoming Wise: A Psycho-Gerontological Interpretation of the *Book of Job*." *International Journal on Aging and Human Development* 32/1 (1991): 21-39.

0957 [Amado] Lévy-Valensi, Éliane. *Job: réponse à Jung* [Parole présente]. Paris: Cerf, 1991.

0958 Collins, Brendan. "Wisdom in Jung's *Answer to Job*." *BTB* 21/3 (1991): 97-101.

0959 Quillo, Ronald. "Naked Am I: Psychological Perspectives on the Unity of the book of Job." *Perspectives in Religious Studies* 18 (1991): 213-222.

0960 Roy, Arlin. "The Book of Job: A Grief and Human Development Interpretation." *Journal of Religion and Health* 30/2 (1991): 149-160.

0961 Scheffler, Eben. "Jung's *Answer to Job*: An Appraisal." *OTE* 4 (1991): 327-341.

0962 Nimmo, Peter W. "Sin, Evil, and Job: Monotheism as a Psychological and Pastoral Problem." *Pastoral Psychology* 42 (July 1994): 427-439.

0963 Or-Bach, Israel. "Job — A Biblical Message About Suicide." *Journal of Psychology and Judaism* 18 (1994): 241-247.

Religion

0964 Brandon, S.G.F. "The Book of Job: Its Significance for the History of Religions." *History Today* 2 (1961): 547-554.

0965 Bakan, D. "Sacrifice and the Book of Job." In *Disease, Pain and Sacrifice*. Chicago 1968, pp. 95-128.

0966 Raphael, D.D. "Tragedy and Religion." In P.S. Sanders (ed.). *Twentieth Century Interpretations of the Book of Job: A Collection of Essays*. Englewood Cliffs: Prentice-Hall, 1968, pp. 46-55.

0967 Brandon, S.G.F. *The Book of Job: Its Significance for the History of Religions*. New York: Scribners, 1969.

0968 Roberts, J.J.M. "Job and the Israelite Religious Tradition." *ZAW* 89 (1977): 107-114.

0969 Maillot, A. "L'apologetique du livre de Job." *RHPR* 59 (1979): 567-576.

0970 MacKenzie, Roderick. "The Cultural and Religious Background of the Book of Job." In C. Duquoc and C. Floristan (eds.). *Job and the Silence of God* [Concilium, 169]. Edinburgh: T&T Clark, 1983, pp. 3-7.

0971 Janzen, J. Gerald. "The Place of the Book of Job in the History of Israel's Religion." In P.D. Miller, et al. (eds.). *Ancient Israelite Religion* [festschrift for Frank Moore Cross]. Philadelphia 1987, pp. 523-537.

0972 Müller, Hans-Peter. "Gottes Antwort an Ijob und das Recht religiöser Wahrheit." *BZ* 32 (1988): 210-231.

Repentance

0973 García-Moreno, A. *Sentido del dolor en Job.* Toledo 1990.

0974 Dailey, Thomas F. "The Aesthetics of Repentance: Re-Reading the Phenomenon of Job." *BTB* 23 (1993): 64-70.

0975 Dailey, Thomas F. *The Repentant Job: A Ricoeurian Icon for Biblical Theology.* Lanham, MD: University Press of America, 1994.

Rhetoric

0976 Loyd, Douglas E. "Patterns of Interrogative Rhetoric in the Book of Job." Dissertation, Iowa, 1986.

0977 Smick, Elmer B. "Architectonics, Structural Poems, and Rhetorical Devices in the Book of Job." In W. Kaiser and R. Youngblood (eds.). *A Tribute to Gleason Archer.* Chicago 1986, pp. 87-104.

0978 Han, Jin Hee. "Yahweh Replies to Job: Yahweh's Speeches in the Book of Job, a Case of Resumptive Rhetoric." Dissertation, Princeton Theological Seminary, 1988.

0979 Koops, Robert. "Rhetorical Questions and Implied Meaning in the Book of Job." *BT* 39 (1988): 415-423.

0980 Ronen, Miriam. "The Hebrew Apologia: Job in the Light of Socrates." Dissertation, New York University, 1991.

0981 van Rensburg, J.F.J. "Wise Men Saying Things by Asking Questions: The Function of the Interrogative in Job 3 to 14." *OTE* 4 (1991): 227-247.

0982 Course, John E. *Speech and Response: A Rhetorical Analysis of the Introductions to the Speeches of the Book of Job, Chapters 4-24* [CBQMS, 25]. Washington, DC: Catholic Biblical Association, 1994.

0983 de Regt, L.J. "Implications of Rhetorical Questions in Strophes in Job 11 and 15." In W. Beuken (ed.), *The Book of Job* [BETL, 114]. Leuven: University Press, 1994, pp. 321-328.

0984 de Regt, Lénart J. "Functions and Implications of Rhetorical Questions in the Book of Job." In Robert D. Bergen (ed.). *Biblical Hebrew and Discourse Linguistics*. Dallas: Summer Institute of Linguistics, 1994, pp. 361-373.

0984a Steinmann, Andrew E. "The Graded Numerical Saying in Job." In Astrid B. Beck, et al. (eds.). *Fortunate the Eyes That See* [festschrift for D.N. Freedman]. Grand Rapids: Eerdmans, 1995, pp. 288-297.

0985 van der Lugt, Pieter. *Rhetorical Criticism and the Poetry of the Book of Job* [OTS, 32]. Leiden: Brill, 1995.

Science

0986 Wolfers, David. "Science in the Book of Job." *Dor le Dor* 19/1 (1990): 18-21.

0987 Strong, David. "The Promise of Technology Versus God's Promise in Job." *TToday* 48 (1991): 170-181.

Septuagint

0988 Ziegler, J. "Der textkritische Word der Septuaginta des Buches Hiob." In *Miscellanea Biblica, 2*. Rome: Biblical Institute, 1934, pp. 277-296.

0989 Gray, J. "The Masoretic Text of the Book of Job, the Targum and the Septuagint Version in the Light of the Qumran Targum (11QTgJob)." *ZAW* 86 (1974): 331-350.

0990 Schaller, Berndt. "Das Testament Hiobs und die Septuaginta-Übersetzung des Buches Hiob." *Bib* 61 (1890): 377-406.

0991 Heater, Homer. *A Septuagint Translation Technique in the Book of Job* [CBQMS, 11]. Washington, DC: Catholic Biblical Association, 1982.

0992 Gammie, John G. "The Angelology and Demonology in the Septuagint of the Book of Job." *HUCA* 56 (1985): 1-19.

0993 Ziegler, Joseph. *Beiträge zum griechischen Iob*. Göttingen: Vandenhoeck and Ruprecht, 1985.

0994 Cimosa, Mario. "L'intercessione di Giobbe in LXX Gb 42,7-10." *Salesianum* 48 (1986): 513-538.

0995 Cox, Claude. "Methodological Issues in the Exegesis of LXX Job." In Claude Cox (ed.). *Sixth Congress of the International Organization for Septuagint and Cognate Studies* [SBLSCS, 23]. Atlanta: Scholars Press, 1987, pp. 79-89.

0996 Gammie, J.G. "The LXX of Job: Its Poetic Style and Relationship to the LXX of Proverbs." *CBQ* 49/1 (1987): 14-31.

0997 Pace, Umberto. "Il LXX di Giobbe: metodologia della versione greca e possibilità di datazione attraverso l'analisi delle techniche di traduzione." *Acme* 45 (1992): 5-24.

0998 Fernandez Marcos, N. "The Septuagint Reading of the Book of Job." In W. Beuken (ed.), *The Book of Job* [BETL, 114]. Leuven: University Press, 1994, pp. 251-266.

0999 Gentry, Peter John. *The Asterisked Material in the Greek Job* [SBLSCS, 38]. Atlanta: Scholars Press, 1995.

Sin

1000 Milgrom, Jacob. "The Cultic *segaga* and Its Influence in Psalms and Job." *JQR* 58/2 (1967): 115-125.

1001 Zink, J.K. "Uncleanness and Sin in Job xiv 4 and Ps xli 7." *VT* 17 (1967): 354-361.

1002 Schmidt, Paul. "Sinnfrage und Glaubenskrise: Ansätze zu einter kritischen Theologie der Schöpfung im Buche Hiob." *Geist und Leben* 45 (1972): 348-363.

1003 Gese, Hartmut. "Die Frage nach dem Lebenssinn: Hiob und die Folgen." *ZTK* 79 (1982): 161-179.

1004 Brown, Walter E. "The Nature of Sin in the Book of Job." Dissertation, New Orleans Baptist Theological Seminary, 1983.

Social Studies

1005 Guillaume, A. "The Arabic Background of the Book of Job." In F.F. Bruce (ed.). *Promise and Fulfillment* [festschrift for S.H. Hooke]. Edinburgh: T & T Clark, 1963, pp. 106-127.

1006 Goodheart, E. "Job and the Modern World." In P.S. Sanders (ed.). *Twentieth Century Interpretations of the Book of Job: A Collection of Essays.* Englewood Cliffs: Prentice-Hall, 1968, pp. 98-106.

1007 Rubenstein, R.L. "Job and Auschwitz." *USQR* 25 (1969): 421-437.

1008 Albertz, Rainer. "Der sozialgeschichtliche Hintergrund des Hiobbuches und der 'Babylonische Theodizee'." In J. Jeremias and L. Perlitt (eds.). *Die Botschaft und die Boten* [festschrift for Hans Walter Wolff]. Neukerchen-Vluyn, 1981, pp. 349-372.

1009 Dion, Paul. "Un nouvel éclairage sur le contexte culturel des malheurs de Job." *VT* 34 (1984): 213-215.

1010 Silbermann, Alphons. "Soziologische Anmerkungen zum Buch Hiob." *ZRGG* 41/1 (1989): 1-11.

1011 Safire, William. *The First Dissident: The Book of Job in Today's Politics.* New York: Random House, 1992.

1012 Newsom, Carol A. "Cultural Politics and the Reading of Job." *Biblical Interpretation* 1 (1993): 119-138.

1013 Berges, U. "Hiob in Lateinamerika: Der leidende Mensch und der aussätzige Gott." In W. Beuken (ed.), *The Book of Job* [BETL, 114]. Leuven: University Press, 1994, pp. 297-320.

1014 Ruíz, Jean-Pierre. "Contexts in Conversation: First World and Third World Readings of Job." *Journal of Hispanic/Latino Theology* 2 (Fall 1995): 5-29.

Soteriology

1015 Mattioli, A. "Le ultime ragioni dell'esistenza del male e sella sofferenza in Giobbe." In *La Sapienza della Croce oggi* 3 (1976): 157-187.

1016 Townsend, T.P. "Soteriology and the Book of Job." *Bible Bhashyam* 14 (1988): 117-131.

1017 Mitchell, Christopher. "Job and the Theology of the Cross." *CJ* 15 (1989): 156-180.

1018 Gilkey, Langdon. "Power, Order, Justice, and Redemption: Theological Comments on Job." In Leo G. Perdue and W. Clark Gilpin (eds.). *The Voice from the Whirlwind: Interpreting the Book of Job*. Nashville: Abingdon Press, 1992, pp. 159-171.

Spirituality

1019 Bogert, Elizabeth A. "The Desolation and Solitude of Job as Postulate of the Essential Creativity of Solitude." *Muslim World* 52 (1962): 322-330.

1020 Lévêque, Jean. "Job. ou l'espoir déraciné." *VSpir* 125 (1971): 287-304.

1021 Vogels, Walter. "The Spiritual Growth of Job: A Psychological Approach to the Book of Job." *BTB* 11 (July 1981): 77-80.

1022 Beck, Harrell F. "Maturity, Spirituality and the Bible: Job's Search for Integrity." In Charles Kao (ed.). *Maturity and the Quest for Spiritual Meaning*. Lanham, MD: University Press of America, 1988, pp. 53-63.

1023 Ravasi, Gianfranco. " 'Ora i miei occhi ti vedono': l'itinerario spirituale di Giobbe." In L. Bouyer (ed.). *Storia della Spiritualità*. Bologna: Dehoniane, 1988, pp. 604-626.

1024 Dietrich, Luiz José. "Jó: uma espiritualidade para sujeitos históricos." *EstBib* 30 (1991): 32-43.

1025 Dailey, Thomas F. "Seeing He Repents: Contemplative Consciousness and the Wisdom of Job." *American Benedictine Review* 46 (1995): 87-101.

1026 Pretorius, P.A.C. "Die geestelike oorlog as hermeneutiese beginsel geïllustreer aan die hand van Job." *Nederduits Gereformeerde Teologiese Tydskrif* 35 (1994): 469-474.

1026a Luebering, Carol. *A Retreat with Job and Julian of Norwich.* Cincinnati: St. Anthony Messenger Press, 1995.

1027 Chieregatti, Arrigo. *Giobbe: lettura spirituale* [Conversazioni bibliche]. Bologna: EDB, 1995.

Structure

1028 Feinberg, Charles L. "The Poetic Structure of the Book of Job and Ugaritic Literature." *BSac* 103 (1946): 283-292.

1029 Fohrer, Georg. "Der innere Aufbau des Buches Hiob." *TZ* 15 (1959): 1-21.

1030 Skehan, Patrick W. "Strophic Patterns in the Book of Job." *CBQ* 23 (1961): 125-141.

1031 Kissane, Edward. "The Metrical Structure of Job." In P.S. Sanders (ed.). *Twentieth Century Interpretations of the Book of Job: A Collection of Essays.* Englewood Cliffs: Prentice-Hall, 1968, pp. 78-85.

1032 Hirsh, N.D. "The Architecture of the Book of Job." *Central Conference of American Rabbis Journal* 16/1 (1969): 22-32.

1033 Laurin, Robert. "The Theological Structure of Job." *ZAW* 84 (1972): 86-89.

1034 Polzin, Robert. "The Framework of the Book of Job." *Int* 28 (1974): 182-200.

1035 Westermann, Claus. *Der Aufbau des Buches Hiob.* Stuttgart 1977.

1036 Reddy, Mummadi Prakasa. "The Book of Job — A Reconstruction." *ZAW* 90 (1978): 59-94.

1037 Sawyer, J.F.A. "The Authorship and Structure of the Book of Job." In E. Livinstone (ed.). *Studia Biblica, I* [6th International Congress on Biblical Studies]. Sheffield: University, 1979, pp. 253-257.

1038 Vogels, Walter. "Job a parlé correctement -- une approche structurale du livre de Job." *NRT* 102 (1980): 835-852.

1039 Hoffman, Yair. "The Relation between the Prologue and the Speech Cycles in Job: A Reconsideration." *VT* 31 (1981): 160-170.

1040 Parsons, Gregory W. "The Structure and Purpose of the Book of Job." *BSac* 138 (1981): 139-157.

1041 Vogels, Walter. "The Spiritual Growth of Job: A Psychological Approach to the Book of Job." *BTB* 11 (July 1981): 77-80.

1042 Westermann, Claus. *The Structure of the Book of Job: A Form-Critical Analysis*. Philadelphia: Fortress Press, 1981.

1043 Bowes, Paula J. "The Structure of Job." *TBT* 20 (1982): 329-333.

1044 Nicholls, Peter H. "The Structure and Purpose of the Book of Job." Dissertation, Hebrew University, 1982.

1045 Vogels, Walter. "The Analysis of a Book: The Book of Job." *Reading and Preaching the Bible: A New Semiotic Approach* [Background Books, 4]. Wilmington: Michael Glazier, 1986, pp. 80-106.

1046 Cox, Dermot. "The Book of Job as 'Bipolar *Mašal*': Structure and Interpretation." *Anton* 62 (1987): 12-25.

1047 Fontaine, Carole. "Folkstale Structure in the Book of Job: A Formalist Reading." In E.R. Follis (ed.). *Directions in Biblical Hebrew Poetry* [JSOTSup, 40]. Sheffield: Almond Press, 1987, pp. 205-232.

1048 van der Lugt, Pieter. "Strophes and Stanzas in the Book of Job: A Historical Survey." In W. van der Meer (ed.). *The Structural Analysis of Biblical and Canaanite Poetry* [JSOTSup, 74]. Sheffield 1988, pp. 235-264.

1049 Erikson, Gösta and Kristina Jonasson. "Jobsbokens juridiska grundmönster." *STK* 65/2 (1989): 64-69.

1050 Miller, Ward S. "The Structure and Meaning of Job." *Concordia Journal* 15 (1989): 103-120.

1051 Seitz, C.R. "Job: Full Structure, Movement and Interpretation." *Int* 43 (1989): 5-17.

1052 Alexander, Jon. "Job Considered as a Conversion Account." *Spirituality Today* 42 (1990): 126-140.

1053 Quillo, Ronald. "Naked Am I: Psychological Perspectives on the Unity of the Book of Job." *Perspectives in Religious Studies* 18 (1991): 213-222.

1054 Joosten, J. "La macrostructure du livre de Job et quelques parallèles (Jérémie 45; 1 Rois 19)." In W. Beuken (ed.), *The Book of Job* [BETL, 114]. Leuven: University Press, 1994, pp. 400-404.

1055 Steinmann, Andrew E. "The Structure and Message of the Book of Job." *VT* 46 (1996): 85-100.

Suffering

1056 Thompson, Kenneth. "Out of the Whirlwind: The Sense of Alienation in the Book of Job." *Int* 14 (1960): 51-63.

1057 Steinmann, J. *Job, témoin de la souffrance humaine* [Foi vivante, 120]. Paris: Cerf, 1969.

1058 Bennett, T.M. "When a Righteous Man Suffers." *SWJT* 14 (1971): 57-64,

1059 Kutsch, E. "Hiob: leidender Gerechter - leidender Mensch." *KD* 19 (1973): 197-214.

1060 von Rad, Gerhard. "Die Diskussion über die Leiden Hiobs." In O.H. Steck (ed.). *Gottes Wirken in Israel*. Neukirchen 1974, pp. 85-90.

1061 von Rad, Gerhard. "Die Erzählung von den Leiden Hiobs." In O.H. Steck (ed.). *Gottes Wirken in Israel*. Neukirchen 1974, pp. 79-84.

1062 Kahn, J.H. *Job's Illness: Loss, Grief and Integretation. A Psychological Interpretation*. New York: Pergamon, 1975.

1063 Lévêque, Jean. "Le sens de la souffrance d'après le livre de Job." *RTL* 6 (1975): 438-459.

1064 Mattioli, A. "Le ultime ragioni dell'esistenza del male e sella sofferenza in Giobbe." In *La Sapienza della Croce oggi* 3 (1976): 157-187.

1065 Ruprecht, E. "Leiden und Gerechtigkeit bei Hiob." *ZTK* 73 (1976): 424-445.

1066 Lévêque, Jean. "Souffrance et métamorphose de Job." *Communio* 2/3 (May 1977): 6-16.

1067 Häring, Hermann. "Ijob in unserer Zeit: zum Problem des Leiden in der Welt." In Theodor Schneider (ed.). *Vorsehungund Handeln Gottes* [QD, 115]. Friburg: Herder, 1988, pp. 168-191.

1068 Sheldon, Mark. "Job, Human Suffering, and Knowledge: Some Contemporary Jewish Perspectives." *Encounter* 41 (1980): 229-235.

1069 Tengbom, Mildred. *Sometimes I Hurt: Reflections and Insights from the Book of Job*. Nashville: Nelson, 1980.

1070 Pipes, Buddy R. "Christian Response to Human Suffering: A Lay Theological Response to the Book of Job." Dissertation, Drew University (Madison, NJ) 1981.

1071 Stedman, Ray C. *Expository Studies in Job: Behind Suffering*. Waco: Word, 1981.

1072 Zenger, Erich. *Durchkreuztes Leben: Hiob, Hoffnung für die Leidenden verkürzt.* Freiburg: Herder, 1981.

1073 Archer, Gleason L. *The Book of Job: God's Answer to the Problem of Undeserved Suffering.* Grand Rapids: Baker, 1982.

1074 Kubina, Veronika. "Ja-Sagen zur Wirklichkeit: Leiden und Leidbewältigung im Buche Ijob." *Katechetische Blätter* 107 (1982): 743-753.

1075 Zenger, E. "Ijob - ein Lebensbuch für Leidende und Mitleidende." *Lebendige Katechese* 5 (1983): 106-110.

1076 Zahrnt, Heinz. *Wie kann Gott das zulassen? Hiob - der Mensch im Leid.* München: Piper, 1985.

1077 Alonso Schökel, Luis. "Giobbe, la crisi della teologia; Giobbe, il mistero della sofferenza." In the *Atti 5° Convegno di Aggiornamento Biblico-Pastorale per Sacerdoti.* Sacile: Centro di Studi Biblici, 1986, pp. 55-78.

1078 Gutiérrez, Gustavo. *On Job: God-Talk and the Suffering of the Innocent.* Maryknoll, NY: Orbis Books, 1987.

1079 Schimmel, Sol. "Job and the Psychology of Suffering and Doubt." *Journal of Psychology and Judaism* 11 (1987): 239-249.

1080 Corey, Lawrence. "The Paradigm of Job." *Dor le Dor* 17/2 (1988-89): 121-128.

1081 Van Praag, Herman M. "Job's Agony: A Biblical Evocation of Bereavement and Grief." *Judaism* 37 (1988): 173-187.

1082 Raabe, Paul R. "Human Suffering in Biblical Context." *Concordia Journal* 15/2 (1989): 139-155.

1082a Rohr, Richard. "Interpreting the Book of Job: Meaning in the Midst of Suffering." *Living Prayer* 22 (1989): 3-9.

1083 Bonora, Antonio. *Giobbe: il tormento di credere.* Il problema e lo scandolo del dolore. Padova: Gregoriana Libreria Editrice, 1990.

1084 García-Morena, Antonio. *Sentido del dolor en Job.* Toledo: S. Ildefonso, 1990.

1085 Martini, Carlo Maria. *Avete perseverato con me nelle mie prove: riflessioni su Giobbe.* Casala Monferrato: Piemme, 1990.

1086 Atkinson, David. *The Message of Job: Suffering and Grace.* Intervarsity Press, 1991.

1087 Dittrich, William F. "An Experience of Developing Relationship: the Book of Job." *TBT* 29 (1991): 169-174.

1088 Sánchez, B. Galo. "Job o el sufrimento abierto al misterio." *Theologica Xaviernia* 41 (1991): 173-183.

1089 Schulz, Karl A. *Where Is God When You Need Him?* Sharing Stories of Suffering with Job and Jesus: From Easy Answers to Hard Questions. New York: Alba House, 1991.

1090 Williams, James G. "Job and the God of Victims." In Leo G. Perdue and W. Clark Gilpin (eds.). *The Voice from the Whirlwind: Interpreting the Book of Job.* Nashville: Abingdon Press, 1992, pp. 208-231.

1091 Hyman, Frieda Clark. "Job, or the Suffering of God." *Judaism* 42/2 (1993): 218-228.

1092 Moore, Michael S. "Job's Texts of Terror." *CBQ* 55 (1993): 662-675.

1093 Kushner, Harold S. "Why Bad Things Happen: Lessons from the Book of Job." *Areopagus* 7/1 (1994): 10-12.

1094 Pleins, J. David. "Why Do You Hide Your Face?" *Int* 48 (1994): 229-238.

1095 Spangenberg, I.J.J. "Om te teologiseer oor God en lyding: Opmerkings na aanleiding van Harold Kushner se interpretasie van Job 40:9-14." *HerTS* 50/4 (1994): 990-1004.

1096 Wagner, Siegfried. "Leiderfahrung und Leidbewältigung im biblischen Ijobbuch." In Matthias Albani and Timotheus Arndt (eds.). *Gottes Ehre erzählen* [festschrift for Hans Seidel]. Leipzig: Thomas Verlag, 1994, pp. 185-210.

1097 Cañellas, Gabriel. "¿Por qué sufren los justos?" Respuesta del libro de job." *Biblia y Fe* 62/2 (1995): 26-54.

1098 Lamb, Jonathan. *The Rhetoric of Suffering: Reading the Book of Job in the Eighteenth Century*. Cambridge: Oxford University Press, 1995.

1098a Tai, Nicholas H.F. and Peter K.H. Lee. "A Dialogue: Job, Paul, and the Chinese Sages on Suffering." *Theology and Life* 17-19 (1996): 179-195.

1099 Thomason, Bill. *God on Trial: The Book of Job and Human Suffering*. Collegeville: Lilturgical Press, 1997.

Targums

1100 Jongeling, B. "Contributions of the Qumran Job Targum to the Aramaic Vocabulary." *JSS* 17/2 (1972): 191-197.

1101 Kaufman, Stephen A. "The Job Targum from Qumran." *JAOS* 93 (1973): 317-327.

1102 Morrow, Francis J. "11Q Targum Job and the Masoretic Text." *RevQ* 8/30 (1973): 253-256.

1103 York, A.D. "A Philological and Textual Analysis of the Qumran Job Targum (11QtgJob)." Dissertation, Cornell University, 1973.

1104 Andersen, Francis I. "The Qumran Targum of Job." *BurH* 10/3 (1974): 77-84.

1105 Caquot, A. "Un écrit sectair de Qumrân: Le 'Targum' de Job." *RHR* 185 (1974): 9-27.

1106 Fitzmyer, Joseph A. "Some Observations on the Targum of Job from Qumran Cave XI." *CBQ* 36 (1974): 503-524.

1107 Gray, J. "The Masoretic Text of the Book of Job, the Targum and the Septuagint Version in the Light of the Qumran Targum (11QTgJob)." *ZAW* 86 (1974): 331-350.

1108 Jongeling, B. "La Colonne XVI de 11Qtg Job." *RevQ* 8/31 (1974): 415-416.

1109 Jongeling, B. *Eenaramees Boek Job*. Amsterdam: Bolland, 1974.

1110 Sokoloff, M. *The Targum to Job from Qumrn Cave XI* [Bar-Ilan Studies in Eastern Languages and Literature]. Ramat-Gan: Bar-Ilan University, 1974.

1111 Weiss, Raphael. "Further Notes on the Qumran Targum to Job." *JSS* 19 (1974): 13-18.

1112 Weiss, Raphael. "The Aramaic Targum of Job." Dissertation, Hebrew University, 1974.

1113 García, Florentino. "Neuvas Lecturas de 11QtgJob." *Sef* 36 (1976): 241-249.

1114 Borger, R. "Hiob xxxix 23 nach dem Qumran-Targum." *VT* 27 (1977): 102-105.

1115 Brownlee, W.H. "The Cosmic Rule of Angels in the 11Q Targum of Job." *JSJ* v8 (1977): 83-84.

1116 Muraoka, T. "Notes on the Old Targum of Job from Qumran Cave XI." *RevQ* 9/33 (1977): 117-125.

1117 Vasholtz, R.I. "Two Notes on 11QtgJob and Biblical Aramaic." *RevQ* 10 (1979): 93s.

1118 Weiss, Raphael. *The Aramaic Targum of Job* [Chaim Rosenberg School for Jewish Studies]. Tel Aviv University, 1979.

1119 Zuckerman, Bruce. "For Your Sake: A Case Study in Aramaic Semantics (11 QtgJob 1:7)." *JANES* 15 (1983): 119-129.

1120 Mastin, Brian. "A Re-Examination of an Alleged Orthographic Feature in 4 Q Targum Job." *RevQ* 11/4 (1984): 583-584.

1121 Aufrecht, W.E. *A Bibliography on the Job Targumim* [NewsTargCog, 3]. Toronto: University Near East Studies, 1987.

1122 Zuckerman, Bruce. "The Date of 11Q Targum Job: A Paleographic Consideration of Its Vorlage." *JSP* 1 (1987): 57-78.

1123 Mangan, Céline. *The Targum of Job* [Aramaic Bible, 15]. London: T&T Clark, 1991.

1124 Mangan, C. "The Interpretation of Job in the Targums." In W. Beuken (ed.), *The Book of Job* [BETL, 114]. Leuven: University Press, 1994, pp. 267-280.

1125 Stec, David M. "The Recent English Translation of the Targumim to Job, Proverbs and Qohelet: A Review." *JSS* 39 (1994): 161-181.

1126 Stec, David M. *The Text of the Targum of Job: An Introduction and Critical Edition* [AGJU, 20]. Leiden: Brill, 1994.

Testament of Job

1127 Delcor, Mathias. "Le Testament de Job, la prière de Nabonide et les traditions targoumiques." In Siegfried Wagner (ed.). *Bibel und Qumran: Beitrage zur Erforschung der Beziehungen zwischen Bibel- und Qumranwissenschaft*. Berlin: Evangelische Haput-Bibelgessellchaft, 1968, pp. 57-74.

1128 Jacobs, Irving. "Literary Motifs in the Testament of Job." *JJS* 21 (1970): 1-10.

1129 Rahnenführer, Dankwart. "Das Testament des Hiob und das Neue Testament." *ZNW* 62 (1971) 68-93.

1130 Collins, John J. "Structure and Meaning in the Testament of Job." In George W. MacRae (ed.). *SBLSP*, 1974, vol. I, pp. 35-52.

1131 Kee, Howard C. "Satan, Magic, and Salvation in the Testament of Job." In George W. MacRae (ed.). *SBLSP*, 1974, vol. I, pp. 53-76.

1132 Schaller, Berndt. "Das Testament Hiobs und die Septuaginta-Übersetzung des Buches Hiob." *Bib* 61 (1890): 377-406.

1133 van der Horst, Pieter. "The Role of Women in the Testament of Job." *NedTTs* 40 (1986): 273-289.

1134 Knibb, Michael A. and Pieter van der Horst (eds.). *Studies on the Testament of Job* [SNTSMS, 66]. Cambridge: Cambridge University Press, 1989.

1135 Schaller, Berndt. "Zur Komposition und Konzeption des Testaments Hiobs." In In M. Knibb and P. van der Horst (eds.). *Studies on the Testament of Job* [SNTSMS, 66]. Cambridge: Cambridge University Press, 1989, pp. 46-92.

1135a Spittler, Russell P. "The Testament of Job: A History of Research and Interpretation." In M. Knibb and P. van der Horst (eds.). *Studies on the Testament of Job* [SNTSMS, 66]. Cambridge: Cambridge University Press, 1989, pp. 7-32.

1136 Seidel, Hans. "Hiob, der Patron der Musiker." In Jutta Hausmann and Hans J. Zobel (eds.). *Alttestamentlicher Glaube und biblische Theologie* [festschrift for Horst Deitrich Preuss]. Stuttgart: Kohlhammer, 1992, pp. 225-232.

1137 Garrett, Susan R. "The 'Weaker Sex' in the Testament of Job." *JBL* 112 (1993): 55-70.

1138 Wahl, Harald Martin. "Elihu, Frevler oder Frommer? Die Audlegung des Hiobbuches (HI 32-37) durch ein Pesudepigraphon (TestHi 41-43)." *JSJ* 25 (June 1994): 1-17.

Theodicy

1139 Stamm, Johann J. "Die Theodizee in Babylon und Israel." *JEOL* 9 (1944): 99-107.

1140 Stockhammer, M. *Das Buch Hiob: Versuch einer Theodizee*

1141 Raurell, Frederic. "Ètica de Job i llibertat de Déu." *Revista Catalana de Teología* 4 (1979): 5-24.

1142 O'Connor, Daniel J. "Theodicy in the Whirlwind." *ITQ* 54 (1988): 161-174.

1143 Horne, Milton P. "Theodicy and the Problem of Human Surrender in Job." Dissertation, Oxford, 1989.

1144 Mattingly, Gerald L. "The Pious Sufferer: Mesopotamia's Traditional Theodicy and Job's Counselors." In William Hallo, Bruce Jones, and Gerald Mattingly (eds). *The Bible in the Light of Cuneiform Literature*. Lewiston, NY: Edwin Mellen, 1990, pp. 305-348.

1145 Theobald, Gerd. "Hiobs Prozess und Gottes Gerecht: die poetische Theodizee des Welttheaters." Dissertation, Heidelberg, 1991.

1146 Tilley, Terrence. "Considering Job: Does Job Fear God for Naught?" *The Evils of Theodicy*. Washington, DC: Georgetown University Press, 1991, pp. 89-112.

1147 Müller, Hans-Peter. "Theodizee? Anschlusserörterungen zum Buch Hiob." *ZTK* 89 (1992): 249-279.

1148 Brandle, Werner. "Hiob - ein tragischer Held? Uberlegungen zur theodizeethematik der Hiobdichtung." *KD* 39/4 (1993): 282-292.

1149 Theobald, Gerd. *Hiobs Botschaft: Die Ablösung der metaphysischen durch die poetische Theodizee*. Gütersloh: Kaiser, 1993.

1150 Nicholson, E.W. "The Limits of Theodicy as a Theme in the Book of Job." In John Day, Robert Gordon, and H. Williamson (eds.). *Wisdom in Ancient Israel* [festschrift for J.A. Emerton]. Cambridge/New York: Cambridge University Press, 1995, pp. 71-82.

Theology

1151 Knight, Harold. "Job, Considered as a Contribution to Hebrew Theology." *SJT* 9 (1956): 63-76.

1152 Taylor, William S. "Theology and Therapy in Job." *TToday* 12 (1956): 451-462.

1153 Larue, Gerald. "The Book of Job on the Futility of Theological Discussion." *The Personalist* 45 (1964): 72-79.

1154 von Rohr Sauer, Alfred. "Salvation by Grace: The Heart of Job's Theology." *Concordia Theological Monthly* 37 (1966): 259-270.

1155 Kaiser, Otto. "Leid und Gott: Ein Beitrag zur Theologie des Buches Hiob." In *Sichtbare Kirche* [festschrift for H. Laag]. Gütersloh: Mohn, 1973, pp. 13-21.

1156 Pixley, J.V. "Jób, ou o diálogo sobre a razâo teológica." *Cuadernos de Teología* 3 (1973): 57-80.

1157 Pixley, J.V. "La ironía antesala de la teología de la liberacíon: el libro de Job." *Cuadernos de Teología* 3 (1973): 57-80.

1158 Maillot, A. "L'apologetique du livre de Job." *RHPR* 59 (1979): 567-576.

1159 Severino Croatto, J. "El libro de Job como clave herméneutica de la teología." *RevistB* 43 (1981): 33-45.

1160 Alonso Schökel, Luis. "Giobbe, la crisi della teologia; Giobbe, il mistero della sofferenza." In the *Atti 5° Convegno di Aggiornamento Biblico-Pastorale per Sacerdoti*. Sacile: Centro di Studi Biblici, 1986, pp. 55-78.

1161 Perdue, Leo G. *Wisdom in Revolt: Metaphorical Theology in the Book of Job* [JSOTSup, 112]. Sheffield: Almond Press, 1991.

1162 Gilkey, Langdon. "Power, Order, Justice, and Redemption: Theological Comments on Job." In Leo G. Perdue and W. Clark Gilpin (eds.). *The Voice from the Whirlwind: Interpreting the Book of Job*. Nashville: Abingdon Press, 1992, pp. 159-171.

1163 Smith, Gary V. "Is There a Place for Job's Wisdom in Old Testament Theology?" *Trinity Journal* 13 (1992): 3-20.

1164 Levoratti, Armando J. "Las Preguntas de Job." *RevistB* 55 (1993): 1-53.

1165 Theobald, Gerd. "Von der Biblischen Theologie zur Buch-Theologie: Das Hiobbuch als Vorspiel zu einer christlichen Hermeneutik." *Neue Zeitschrift für Systematische Theologie und Religionsphilosophie* 35/3 (1993): 276-302.

1166 Dailey, Thomas. *The Repentant Job: A Ricoeurian Icon for Biblical Theology.* Lanham, MD: University Press of America, 1994.

1167 Dailey, Thomas F. "Job as an Icon for Theology." *Perspectives in Religious Studies* 23/3 (1997).

Wisdom

1168 Donald, Trevor. "Semantic Field of 'Folly' in Provers, Job, Psalms, and Ecclesiastes." *VT* 13 (1963): 285-292.

1169 Aiura, T. "Wisdom Motifs in the Joban Poem." *Kwansei Gakuin University Annual Studies* 15 (1966): 1-20.

1170 von Rad, Gerhard. "Job 38 and Ancient Eastern Wisdom." In *The Problem of the Hexateuch and Other Essays.* London 1966, pp. 281-291.

1171 Gibbs, P.T. *Job and the Mysteries of Wisdom.* Nashville: Southern, 1967.

1172 Gordis, Robert. "Wisdom and Job." In S. Sandmel (ed.). *Old Testament Issues.* London: SCM, 1969, pp. 213-241.

1173 Bennett, T. Miles. *When Human Wisdom Fails:* An Exposition of the Book of Job. Grand Rapids: Baker, 1971.

1174 Winton-Thomas, Daniel. "Types of Wisdom in the Book of Job." *Indian Journal of Theology* 20 (1971): 157-165.

1175 Zerafa, P. *The Wisdom of God in the Book of Job* [Studia Univ. S. Thomae in Urbe, 8]. Rome 1978.

1176 Craigie, P.C. "Biblical Wisdom in the Modern World, III: Job." *Crux* 16 (1980): 7-10.

1177 Perani, Mauro. "Crisi della Sapienza e ricerca di Dio nel libro di Giobbe." *RivB* 28 (1980): 157-184.

1178 Habel, Norman. "Of Things Beyond Me: Wisdom in the Book of Job." *Currents in Theology and Mission* 10 (1983): 142-154.

1179 Harris, Scott L. "Wisdom or Creation? A New Interpretation of Job." *VT* 33 (1983): 419-427.

1180 Plank, Karl A. "Raging Wisdom: A Banner of Defiance Unfurled." *Judaism* 36 (1987): 323-330.

1181 Warner, Martin. "Job versus His Comforters: Rival Paradigms of Wisdom." *Philosophical Finesse: Studies in the Art of Rational Persuasion*. Oxford: Clarendon Press, 1989, pp. 105-151.

1182 Albertz, Rainer. "The Sage and Pious Wisdom in the Book of Job: The Friends' Perspective." In John G. Gammie and Leo G. Perdue (eds.). *The Sage in Israel and the Ancient Near East*. Winona Lake: Eerdmans, 1990, pp. 243-261.

1183 Terrien, Samuel. "Job as a Sage." In *The Sage in Israel and the Ancient Near East* [ed. J. Gammie and L. Perdue]. Winona Lake: Eisenbrauns, 1990, pp. 231-242.

1184 Achenbaum, W. Andrew and Lucinda Orwoll. "Becoming Wise: A Psycho-Gerontological Interpretation of the *Book of Job*." *International Journal on Aging and Human Development* 32/1 (1991): 21-39.

1185 Collins, Brendan. "Wisdom in Jung's *Answer to Job*." *BTB* 21/3 (1991): 97-101.

1186 Wittenberg, G.H. "Job the Farmer: The Judean *'am-haretz* and the Wisdom Movement." *OTE* 4/2 (1991): 151-170.

1187 Smith, Gary V. "Is There a Place for Job's Wisdom in Old Testament Theology?" *Trinity Journal* 13 (1992): 3-20.

1188 Perdue, Leo G. "Wisdom in the Book of Job." In Leo G. Perdue, Bernard Brandon Scott, and William Johnston Wiseman (eds.). *In Search of Wisdom* [festschrift for John G. Gammie]. Louisville: Westminster/John Knox, 1993, pp. 73-98.

1189 Dailey, Thomas F. "Seeing He Repents: Contemplative Consciousness and the Wisdom of Job." *American Benedictine Review* 46 (1995): 87-101.

1190 Lévêque, Jean. "Sagesse et paradox dans le livre de Job." In Jacques Triblet (ed.). *La sagesse biblique: de l'Ancient au Nouveau Testament* [LD, 160]. Paris: Cerf, 1995, pp. 99-128.

1191 Mulrooney, Joe. "Where Shall Wisdom Be Found, and Where Is the Place of Misunderstanding?" *Month* 28 (1995): 341-344.

Part Three

GENERAL Citations

Translations

Commentaries

General Studies
- books
- articles

Literature Reviews

Collected Editions

Translations

1192 Dobson, J.H. "Translating Job — Prose or Poetry?" *BT* 23 (1972): 243-244.

1193 Neiman, D. *The Book of Job: A Presentation of the Book with Selected Portions Translated from the Original Hebrew Text.* Jerusalem: Massada, 1972.

1194 Gray, J. "The Masoretic Text of the Book of Job, the Targum and the Septuagint Version in the Light of the Qumran Targum (11QTgJob)." *ZAW* 86 (1974): 331-350.

1195 Mitchell, Stephen. *Into the Whirlwind: A Translation of the Book of Job.* Garden City: Doubleday, 1979.

1196 Greenberg, Moshe and Jonas C. Greenfield and Nahum M. Sarna. *The Book of Job: A New Translation according to the Traditional Hebrew Text, with Introductions.* Philadelphia: Jewish Publication Society, 1980.

1197 Heater, Homer. *A Septuagint Translation Technique in the Book of Job* [CBQMS, 11]. Washington, DC: Catholic Biblical Association, 1982.

1198 Mitchell, Stephen. *The Book of Job: Translated with an Introduction.* San Francisco 1987.

1199 Wolfers, David. "The Humpty Dumpty Principle in Biblical Translation." *Dor le Dor* 18 (1989-90): 141-147.

1200 Reyburn, William. *A Handbook on the Book of Job.* New York: United Bible Societies, 1992.

1201 Szpek, Heidi M. *Translation Technique in the Peshitta to Job: A Model for Evaluating a Text with Documentation from the Peshitta to Job* [SBLDS, 137]. Atlanta: Scholars Press, 1992.

Commentaries

1202 Driver, Samuel R. and George B. Gray. *A Critical and Exegetical Commentary on the Book of Job* [ICC]. Edinburgh: T&T Clark, 1921.

1203 Buttenwieser, Moses. *The Book of Job*. New York: MacMillan, 1925.

1204 Kissane, Edward. *The Book of Job: Translated from a Critically Revised Hebrew Text with Commentary*. New York: Sheed and Ward, 1946.

1205 Stier, Fridolin. *Das Buch Ijjob*. München: Kosel, 1954.

1206 Larcher, C. *Le livre de Job* [Bible de Jerusalem]. Paris: Cerf, 1957.

1207 Terrien, Samuel. "Job — Introduction and Exegesis." *IB*, 3:877-1198.

1208 Tur-Sinai, N.H. (H. Torczyner). *The Book of Job: A New Commentary*. Jerusalem: Kiryath Sepher, 1957.

1209 Fohrer, Georg. *Das Buch Hiob* [KAT, 16]. Gütersloh: Mohn, 1963.

1210 Terrien, Samuel. *Job* [CAT]. Neuchâtel 1963.

1211 Dhorme, Edouard Paul. *A Commentary on the Book of Job*. London: Thomas Nelson, 1967.

1212 Horst, F. *Hiob I (1-19)*. Neukirchen-Vluyn: Vandenhoeck & Ruprecht, 1968.

1213 Hulme, William E. *Dialogue in Despair: Pastoral Commentary on the Book of Job*. Nashville: Abingdon, 1968.

1214 MacKenzie, R.A.F. "Job." *Jerome Biblical Commentary*, I:511-533.

1215 Weiser, A. *Das Buch Hiob* [ATD, 13]. Göttingen ^{5}1968.

1216 Potter, R. "Job." *New Catholic Commentary on Holy Scripture*. New York, 1969, pp. 417-438.

1217 Hanson, A. *The Book of Job: Introduction and Commentary* [Torch Bible Paperbacks]. London: SCM, 1970.

1218 Fedrizzi, Pio. *Giobbe* [La Sacra Bibbia]. Torino: Marietti, 1972.

1219 von Speyr, A. *Job*. Einsiedeln: Johannes-Verlag, 1972.

1220 Gordis, Robert. "Observations on Problems and Methods in Biblical Research: Writing a Commentary on Job." *PAAJR* 41 (1973): 105-135.

1221 Pope, Marvin H. *Job: Introduction, Translation, and Notes* [AB, 15]. Garden City: Doubleday, '1973.

1222 de Wilde, A. *Het boek Job, ingeleid en vertaald*. Wageningen: Veennan, 1974.

1223 Anderson, Francis I. *Job: An Introduction and Commentary* [TynOTC]. Leicester: Inter-Varsity Press, 1976.

1224 Carlisle, T.J. *Journey with Job*. Grand Rapids: Eerdmans, 1976.

1225 Blei, K. *Job: Verklaring van een Bijbelgedeelte*. Kampen: Kok, 1978.

1226 Gordis, Robert. *The Book of Job: Commentary, New Translation and Special Studies*. New York: KTAV, 1978.

1227 Hesse, Franz. *Hiob* [Züricher Bibel Alten Testament, 14]. Zürich: Theologischer Verlag, 1978.

1228 Zuck, Roy B. *Job* [Everyman's Bible Commentary]. Chicago: Moody, 1978.

1229 Heinan, K. *Der unverfügbare Gott: Das Buch Hiob* [SKKAT 18]. Stuttgart: Katholisches Bibelwerk, 1979.

1230 Fronius, Hans. *Das Buch Hiob*. Klosterneuburg: ÖsKBW, 1980.

1231 de Wilde, Amos. *Das Buch Hiob: eingeleitet, übersetzt und erlautert* [OTS, 22]. Leiden: Brill, 1981.

1232 Bergant, Dianne. *Job, Ecclesiastes* [OTM, 18]. Wilmington: Michael Glazier, 1982.

1233 Martínez, José M. *Job, la fe en conflicto: comentario y reflexiones sobre el libro de Job.* Barcelona: CLIE, 1982.

1234 Pixley, Jorge. *El libro de Job: comentario bíblico latinoamericano.* San José: Sebila, 1982.

1235 Thomas, David. *Book of Job: Expository and Homiletical Commentary.* Grand Rapids: Kregel, 1982.

1236 Alonso Schöke, Luis and José Sicre Díaz. *Job: Comentario teológico y literario.* Madrid: Cristiandad, 1983.

1237 Eaton, J.H. *Job* [OT Guides, 5]. Sheffield: Academic Press, 1985.

1238 Gibson, John C.L. *Job* [Daily Study Bible]. Edinburgh: St. Andrew Press, 1985.

1239 Habel, Norman. *The Book of Job: A Commentary* [OTL]. Philadelphia: Westminster, 1985.

1240 Janzen, J. Gerald. *Job* [IBC]. Atlanta: John Knox, 1985.

1241 van Selms, A. *Job: A Practical Commentary* [Text and Interpretation]. Grand Rapids: Eerdmans, 1985.

1242 Gross, Heinrich. *Ijob* [NEchter AT]. Würzburg: Echter, 1986.

1243 Guinan, Michael D. *Job* [Collegeville Bible Commentary, OT #19]. Collegeville: Liturgical Press, 1986.

1244 McKenna, D.L. *Job* [Communicator's Commentary]. Waco: Word Books, 1986.

1245 Rowley, H.H. *Job* [NCB]. London: Marshall, Morgan & Scott, 1986 (rev. ed.).

1246 Simundson, Daniel J. *The Message of Job: A Theological Commentary* [Augsburg Old Testament Series]. Minneapolis: Augsburg/Fortress, 1986.

1247 Good, Edwin M. "Job." In James L. Mays (ed.). *Harper's Bible Commentary*. San Francisco: Harper and Row, 1988, pp. 407-432.

1248 Hartley, John E. *The Book of Job* [NICOT]. Grand Rapids: Wm. B. Eerdmans, 1988.

1249 Heinen, Karl. *Der unverfügbare Gott: das Buch Ijob* [KlKomm, 18]. Stuttgart: KBW, 1988.

1250 Clines, David J.A. *Job 1-20* [WBC, 17]. Waco, TX: Word Books, 1989.

1251 MacKenzie, R.A.F. and R.E. Murphy. "Job." *NJBC*, pp. 466-488.

1252 Rodd, Cyril. *The Book of Job* [Narrative Bible Commentary]. Philadelphia 1990.

1253 Good, Edwin M. *In Turns of Tempest: A Reading of Job, with a Translation*. Stanford: Stanford University Press, 1991.

1254 Ravasi, Gianfranco. *Giobbe, traduzione e commento*. Roma: Borla, '1991.

1255 Bräumer, Hansjörg. *Das Buch Hiob, erklärt* [Studienbibel AT]. Wurzburg: Brockhaus, 1992.

1256 Lobato Fernández, Jaun Bautista. *El libro de Job, comentario* [Mensaje AT, 18]. Salamanca: Sigueme, 1992.

1257 Alden, Robert L. *Job: An Exegetical and Theological Exposition of Holy Scripture* [New American Commentary, 11]. Nashville: Broadman and Holman, 1993.

1258 Mende, T. *Das Buch Hiob*, Teil II (Kap. 21-42) [Geistliche Schriftlesung, 14/II]. Düsseldorf: Patmos, 1994.

General Studies (books)

1259 Eerdmans, B.D. *Studies in Job*. Leiden 1939.

1260 Gordis, Robert. *The Book of God and Man: A Study of Job*. Chicago: University of Chicago Press, 1965.

1261 Baker, Wesley C. *More Than a Man Can Take: A Study of Job*. Philadelphia: Westminster, 1966.

1262 Jones, Edgar. *The Triumph of Job*. London: SCM, 1966.

1263 Epp, T.H. *Job: A Man Tried as Gold*. Lincoln, NE: Back to the Bible Publications, 1967.

1264 Macbeath, A. *The Book of Job*. Glasgow: Pickering, 1967.

1265 Guillaume, A. *Studies in the Book of Job*, with a New Translation [*ALUOS* Supplement, 2]. Leiden 1968.

1266 Kent, H.H. *Job Our Contemporary*. Grand Rapids: Eerdmans, 1968.

1267 King, H.M. *Songs of the Night: A Study of the Book of Job*. Gerrards Cross: Smythe, 1968.

1268 Snaith, N.H. *The Book of Job:* Its Origin and Purpose [SBT, n.s., 11]. London 1968.

1269 Lévêque, Jean. *Job et son Dieu: Essai d'exégèse et de théologie biblique*, 2 volumes [EBib]. Paris: Gabalda, 1970.

1270 Müller, H.-P. *Hiob und seine Freunde: Traditionsgeschickliches zum Verständnis des Hiobbuches* [ThStud, 103]. Zurich: EVZ-Verlad, 1970.

1271 Bennett, T. Miles. *When Human Wisdom Fails: An Exposition of the Book of Job*. Grand Rapids: Baker, 1971.

1272 Ellison, H.L. *A Study of Job: From Tragedy to Triumph*. Grand Rapids: Zondervan, 1971.

1273 Garland, D.D. *Job: A Study Guide.* Grand Rapids: Zondervan, 1971.

1274 Johnson, L.D. *Out of the Whirlwind: The Major Message of the Book of Job.* Nashville: Boradman, 1971.

1275 Levenson, J.D. *The Book of Job in Its Time and in the Twentieth Century.* London 1972.

1276 Ewing, W.B. *Job: A Vision of God.* New York: Seabury, 1976.

1277 Strauss, James D. *The Shattering of Silence: Job, Our Contemporary* [Bible Study Textbook Series]. Joplin, MO: College Pres, 1976.

1278 Zenger, E. and R. Böswald. *Durchkreuztes Leben: Besinnung auf Hiob.* Freiburg: Herder, 1976.

1279 Frost, G.E. *The Color of the Night: Reflections on the Book of Job.* Minneapolis: Augsburg, 1977.

1280 Job, J. *What Is My Father? The Message of the Book of Job for Christian Today.* London: Epworth, 1977.

1281 Murphy, Roland E. *The Psalms, Job* [OT Witness for Preaching]. Philadelphia 1977.

1282 Rosenberg, David W. *Job Speaks: Interpreted from the Original Hebrew Book of Job* [A Poet's Bible]. New York: Harper and Row, 1977.

1283 Cox, Dermot. *The Triumph of Impotence:* Job and the Tradition of the Absurd [AnGreg, 212]. Roma: PUG, 1978.

1284 Kuhn, Johannes. *Warum bist du so, Gott? Hiob der Fragende.* Stuttgart: Quell, 1978.

1285 Ruckman, Peter S. *The Book of Job.* Pensacola, FL: Pensacola Bible Institute, 1978.

1286 Blackwood, A. *Out of the Whirlwind: A Study of Job.* Grand Rapids: Baker, 1979.

1287 Inch, M. *My Servant Job*. Grand Rapids: Baker, 1979.

1288 Sperka, Joshua S. *The Book of Job — Mankind on Trial: A Modern Interpretation of the Most Perplexing Problem of All Ages*. New York: Bloch, 1979.

1289 Job, John B. *Job Speaks to Us Today*. Atlanta: Knox, 1980.

1290 Marböck, Johannes. *Das Buch Ijob*. Klosterneuburg: Österreichisches Katholisches Bibelwerk, 1980.

1291 Maag, Victor. *Hiob: Wandlung und Verarbeitung des Problems in Novelle, Dialogdichtung und Spätfassungen* [FRLANT, 128]. Göttingen 1982.

1292 Rutler, George W. *The Impatience of Job*. LaSalle, IL: Sugden, 1982.

1293 Deselaers, Paul et al. *Sehnsucht nach dem lebendigen Gott: Das Buch Ijob* [BPrax, 8]. Stuttgart: Katholisches Bibelwerk, 1983.

1294 Fohrer, Georg. *Studien zum Buche Hiob (1956-1979)* [BZAW, 159]. Berlin: Walter de Gruyter, ²1983.

1295 Ravasi, Gianfranco. *Giobbe: il silenzio di Dio*. Roma: Paoline, 1984.

1296 Lévêque, Jean. *Job: le livre et le message* [Cahiers Évangile, 53]. Paris 1985.

1297 Vermeylen, J. *Job, ses amis et son Dieu: le légende de Job et ses relectures postexiliques* [StudBib, 2]. Leiden: Brill, 1986.

1298 Zuckerman, B. *Job the Silent: A Study in Historical Counterpoint*. New York: Oxford University Press, 1989.

1299 Martini, Carlo Maria. *Avete perseverato con me nelle mie prove: riflessioni su Giobbe*. Casala Monferrato: Piemme, 1990.

1300 Penchansky, David. *The Betrayal of God: Ideological Conflict in Job* [Literary Currents in Biblical Interpretation]. Louisville: Westminster/John Knox Press, 1990.

1301 Taylor, David Bruce. *Job: A Rational Exposition*. Braunton Devon: Merlin Books, 1990.

1302 Taylor, David Bruce. *Job: A Rational Exposition*. Braunton-Devon: Merlin Books, 1990.

1303 Atkinson, David. *The Message of Job* [The Bible Speaks Today]. Leicester: Inter-Varsity Press, 1991.

1304 Cox, Dermot. *Man's Anger and God's Silence: The Book of Job*. Middlegreen: St. Paul Publications, 1991.

1305 Wiersbe, Warren W. *Be Patient*. Wheaton, IL: Victor, 1991.

1306 Safire, William. *The First Dissident: The Book of Job in Today's Politics*. New York: Random House, 1992.

1307 Turoldo, David M. *La Parabola di Giobbe* [Quaderni di Ricerca]. Milan: Cooperativa Editrice Nuova Stampa, 1992.

1308 Chiegegatti, Arrigo. *Giobbe, lettura spirituale* [Conversazioni bibliche]. Bologna: EDB, 1995.

1309 Vogels, Walter. *Job, l'homme qui a bien parlé de Dieu*. Paris: Cerf, 1995.

General Studies (articles)

1310 Vischer, Wilhelm. "God's Truth and Man's Lie — A Study in the Message of the Book of Job." *Int* 15 (1961): 131-146.

1311 Pope, Marvin H. "Job, book of." *IDB*, 2: 911-924.

1312 Rowley, H.H. "The Book of Job and Its Meaning." *From Moses to Qumran: Studies in the Old Testament*. London 1963, pp. 141-183.

1313 Tsevat, Matitiahu. "The Meaning of the Book of Job." *HUCA* 37 (1966): 73-106.

1314 Skehan, P.W. "Job, Book of." *NCE* 7 (1967): 999-1001.

1315 Peake, A.S. "The Art of the Book of Job." In P.S. Sanders (ed.). *Twentieth Century Interpretations of the Book of Job: A Collection of Essays.* Englewood Cliffs: Prentice-Hall, 1968, pp. 109-113.

1316 Rexroth, K. "The Book of Job." In P.S. Sanders (ed.). *Twentieth Century Interpretations of the Book of Job: A Collection of Essays.* Englewood Cliffs: Prentice-Hall, 1968, pp. 107-109.

1317 Sewall, R.B. "The Book of Job." In P.S. Sanders (ed.). *Twentieth Century Interpretations of the Book of Job: A Collection of Essays.* Englewood Cliffs: Prentice-Hall, 1968, pp. 21-35.

1318 McKeating, Henry. "The Central Issue of the Book of Job." *ExpTim* 82 (1970): 244-247.

1319 di Nola, A.M. "Giobbe, libro di." *EncRel* 3 (1971): 212-222.

1320 Ginsberg, H.L. "Job, the book of." *EncJud* 10 (1971): 111-129.

1321 Matheney, M.P. "Majors Purposes of the Book of Job." *SWJT* 14 (1971): 17-42.

1322 Smith, E.L. "Introduction to the Book of Job." *SWJT* 14 (1971): 5-16.

1323 Yates, K.M. "Understanding the Book of Job." *RevExp* 68/4 (1971): 443-455.

1324 Schapiro, D.S. "A Study of the Book of Job." *Tradition* 13/2 (1972): 81-99.

1325 Hengstenberg, E.W. "Interpreting the Book of Job." In W.C. Kaiser (ed.). *Classical Evangelical Essays in Old Testament Interpretation.* Grand Rapids: Baker, 1973, pp. 91-112.

1326 Lévêque, Jean and C. Kamnengiesser. "Job (le livre de)." *Dictionnaire de Spiritualité* 8 (1974): 1201-1225.

1327 Payne, J.B. "Inspiration in the Words of Job." In J.H. Skilton (ed.). *The Law and the Prophets* [festschrift for A.T. Allis]. Nutley, NJ: Presbyterian and Reformed Publications, 1974, pp. 319-336.

1328 von Orelli, A. "Hiob: Deutung eines biblischen Mythos." *Reformatio* 25 (1976): 74-82, 148-158.

1329 Zuckerman, B. "Job, book of." *IDBSup*, 479-481.

1330 Robertson, David. "The Book of Job." *The Old Testament and the Literary Critic*. Philadelphia 1977, pp. 33-54.

1331 Scafella, Frank. "A Reading of Job." *JSOT* 14 (1979): 63-67.

1332 Schaller, B. "Berndt, Unterweisung in lehrhafter Form: Das Testament Hiobs." *JSHRZ* 3/3 (1979): 305-387.

1333 Wharton, J.A. "The Unanswerable Answer: An Interpretation of Job." In W.E. March (ed.). *Texts and Testaments: Critical Essays in the Bible and Early Church Fathers* [festschrift for S.D. Currie]. San Antonio: Trinity University Press, 1980, pp. 37-70.

1334 Dornisch, Loretta. "The Book of Job and Ricoeur's Hermeneutics." *Semeia* 19 (1981): 3-22.

1335 Jacobson, Richard. "Satanic Semiotics, Jobian Jurisprudence." *Semeia* 19 (1981): 63-71.

1336 Höffken, Peter. "Hiob in exegetischer Sicht." *Der evangelische Erzieher* 36 (1984): 509-526.

1337 Loader, J.A. "Job — Answer or Enigma?" *OTE* 2 (1984): 1-38.

1338 de Rouville, Odile. "Job dépose son bilan: lecture biblique marginale." *Foi et Vie* 84/6 (1985): 57-66.

1339 DiLella, Alexander. "An Existential Interpretation of Job." *BTB* 15 (1985): 49-55.

1340 Peake, A.S. "Job: The Problem of the Book." In James L. Crenshaw (ed.). *Theodicy in the Old Testament* [Issues in Religion and Theology, 4]. Philadelphia: Fortress Press, 1983, pp. 100-108.

1341 Ebach, Jürgen. "Hiob, Hiobbuch." *TRE* 15 (1986): 360-380.

1342   Smick, Elmer B. "Semiological Interpretation of the Book of Job." *WTJ* 46 (1986): 135-149.

1343   Freedman, David N. "Is It Possible to Understand the Book of Job?" *BRev* 4,3 (1988): 26-33.

1344   Heckelman, Joseph. "The Liberation of Job." *Dor le Dor* 17/1 (1988-89): 128-132.

1345   Long, T.G. "Job: Second Thoughts in the Land of Uz." *TToday* 75 (1988): 5-20.

1346   Yancey, Philip. "A Fresh Reading of the Book of Job." In Roy B. Zuck (ed.). *Sitting with Job: Selected Studies on the Book of Job*. Grand Rapids: Baker, 1992, pp. 141-149.

1347   Clines, David J.A. "Job." In B.W. Anderson (ed.). *The Books of the Bible*, I: The Old Testament/The Hebrew Bible. New York 1989, pp. 181-201.

1348   Clines, David J.A. "Deconstructing the Book of Job." *What Does Eve Do to Help? and Other Readerly Questions to the Old Testament* [JSOTSup, 94]. Sheffield: Almond Press, 1990, pp. 106-123.

1349   Neri, P. "Nota: Chiave di lettura del libro di Giobbe." *BeO* 164 (1990): 102.

1350   Breitbart, Sidney. "The Problem of Job: The Question Still Remains." *JBQ* 20 (1991-92): 105-110.

1351   Dittrich, William F. "An Experience of Developing Relationship: The Book of Job." *TBT* 29 (1991): 169-174.

1352   Potter, Harry. "Rebel against the Light: Job or God." *ExpTim* 103 (1991): 198-201.

1353   West, Gerald. "Hearing Job's Wife: Towards a Feminist Reading of Job." *OTE* 4 (1991): 107-131.

1354   Crenshaw, James L. "Job, book of." *Anchor Bible Dictionary* 3 (1992): 858-868.

1355 Gustafson, James M. "A Response to the Book of Job." In Leo G. Perdue and W. Clark Gilpin (eds.). *The Voice from the Whirlwind: Interpreting the Book of Job*. Nashville: Abingdon Press, 1992, pp. 172-184.

1356 Hunter, Alistair G. "Could Not the Universe Have Come into Existence 200 Yards to the Left? A Thematic Study of Job." In Robert P. Carroll (ed.). *Text and Pretext* [festschrift for Robert Davidson; JSOTSup, 138]. Sheffield: JSOT Press, 1992, pp. 140-159.

1357 Pyper, Hugh. "The Reader in Pain: Job as Text and Pretext." In Robert P. Carroll (ed.). *Text and Pretext* [festschrift for Robert Davidson; JSOTSup, 138]. Sheffield: JSOT Press, 1992, pp. 234-255.

1358 Simundson, Daniel J. "Job and His Ministers." In Arland J. Hultgren, et al. (eds.). *All Things New* [festschrift for Roy A. Harrisville; Word and World Supplement Series, 1]. St. Paul: Word and World, 1992, pp. 33-42.

1359 Bakon, Shimon. "God and Man on Trial." *JBQ* 21 (1993): 226-235.

1360 Green, Barbara. "Recasting a Classic: A Reconsideration of the Meaning of the Book of Job." *NBl* 74 (1993): 213-221.

1361 Levoratti, Armando J. "Las Preguntas de Job." *RevistB* 55 (1993): 1-53.

1362 Millard, Matthias. "Das Hiobbuch. Skizzen zur Interpretation eines Buches der 'Schriften'." *WD* 22 (1993): 27-38.

1363 Newsom, Carol A. "Cultural Politics and the Reading of Job." *Biblical Interpretation* 1 (1993): 119-138.

1364 Wolfers, David. "Job: A Universal Drama." *JBQ* 21 (1993): 13-23, 80-89.

1365 Clines, D.J.A. "Why Is There a Book of Job and What Does It Do to You if You Read It?" In W. Beuken (ed.), *The Book of Job* [BETL, 114]. Leuven: University Press, 1994, pp. 1-20.

1366 Laeuchli, Samuel and Arvind Sharma. "The Problem of Job: An Eastern Response." *ARC* (Journal of the Faculty of Religious Studies, McGill University) 22 (1994): 83-90.

1367 Raurell, F. "The Book of Job." *Estudios Franciscanos* 95 (1994): 493-523.

1368 Bechtel, L. "A Feminist Approach to the Book of Job." In Athalya Brenner (ed.). *A Feminist Companion to Wisdom Literature* [The Feminist Companion to the Bible, 9]. Sheffield: Sheffield Academic Press, 1995, pp. 222-251.

1369 Clines, David J.A. "Deconstructing the Book of Job." *BRev* 11/2 (1995): 30-35, 43-44.

1370 Klein, L. "Job and the Womb: Text about Men, Subtext about Women." In Athalya Brenner (ed.). *A Feminist Companion to Wisdom Literature* [The Feminist Companion to the Bible, 9]. Sheffield: Sheffield Academic Press, 1995, pp. 186-200.

1371 Wolfers, David. "The Book of Job: Its True Significance." *JBQ* 24 (1996): 3-8.

Literature Reviews

1372 Kuhl, Curt. "Neuere Literarkritik des Buches Hiob." *TRu* 21 (1953): 163-205, 257-313.

1373 Kuhl, Curt. "Vom Hiobbuche und seinen Problemen." *TRu* 22 (1954): 261-316.

1374 Glatzer, Nahum N. "The Book of Job and Its Interpreters." *Biblical Motifs: Origins and Transformations* [Philip W. Lown Institute of Advanced Judaic Studies, Studies & Texts, 3]. Cambridge 1966, pp. 197-220.

1375 Barr, James. "The Book of Job and Its Modern Interpreters." *BJRL* 54 (1971): 28-46.

1376 Müller, Hans-Peter. "Altes und Neues zum Buch Hiob." *EvT* 37 (1977): 284-304.

1377 Gelber, S. Michael. "The Book of Job: A Review Essay." *Conservative Judaism* 35/1 (1981): 69-76.

1378 Kinet, Dirk. "Der Vorwurf an Gott. Neuere Literartur zum Ijobbuch." *BK* 36 (1981): 255-259.

1379 Conte, Ginno. "Letture di Giobbe." *Protestantesimo* 39 (1984): 93-96.

1380 Williams, Ronald J. "Current Trends in the Study of the Book of Job." In W. Aufrecht (ed.). *Studies in the Book of Job* [*SR* Sup, 16]. Waterloo, Ont: W. Laurier University, 1985, pp. 1-27.

1380a Rodd, C.S. "Which Is the Best Commentary on Job?" *ExpTim* 97 (1986): 356-359.

1381 Hermisson, Hans-Jürgen. "Notizen zu Hiob." *ZTK* 86 (1989): 125-139.

1382 Ceresko, Anthony R. "Gustavo Gutiérrez, *On Job*: Some Questions of Method." *Indian Theological Studies* 29 (1992): 223-233.

1383 Lavoie, Jean-Jacques. "Les livres de Job, Qohélet et Proverbes: les enjeux méthodologiques dans l'histoire de la recherche depuis 1980." In Michel Gourges and Léo Laberge (eds.). *"De bien des manières": la recherche biblique aux abods due XXe siècle* [LD, 163]. Montreal: Fides, 1995, pp. 147-180.

Collected Editions

1384 Sanders, P.S. (ed.). *Twentieth Century Interpretations of the Book of Job. A Collection of Critical Essays.* Englewood Cliffs: Prentice-Hall, 1968.

1385 Glatzer, Nahum N. (ed.). *The Dimensions of Job:* A Study and Selected Readings. New York: Schocken, 1969.

1386 Polzin, Robert and David Robertson (eds.). *Studies in the Book of Job* [Semeia, 7]. Missoula: Scholars Press, 1977.

1387 Crossan, John Dominic (ed.). *The Book of Job and Ricoeur's Hermeneutics* [Semeia, 19]. Chico, CA: Scholars Press, 1981.

1388 Duquoc, C. and C. Floristan (eds.). *Job and the Silence of God* [Concilium, 169]. Edinburgh: T&T Clark, 1983.

1389 Fohrer, Georg. *Studien zum Buche Hiob (1956-1979)* [BZAW, 159]. Berlin: de Gruyter, 1983.

1390 Perdue, Leo G. and W. Clark Gilpin (eds.). *The Voice from the Whirlwind: Interpreting the Book of Job*. Nashville: Abingdon Press, 1992.

1391 Zuck, Roy B. (ed.). *Sitting with Job: Selected Studies on the Book of Job*. Grand Rapids: Baker, 1992.

1392 Beuken, Willem A.M. (ed.). *The Book of Job* [BETL, 114]. Leuven: University Press, 1994.

1393 Wolfers, David. *Deep Things Out of Darkness — The Book of Job: Essays and a New English Translation*. Winona Lake: Eerdmans, 1995.

AUTHOR Index

Achenbaum, W., 0956, 1184
Ahroni, R., 0678
Aiura, T., 0836, 1169
Albertson, R.G., 0598
Albertz, R., 0517, 0597, 1008, 1182
Albright, W.F., 0510
Alden, R.L., 1257
Alexander, J., 0682, 1052
Alonso Díaz, J., 0693
Alonso Schökel, L., 0358, 0676, 1077, 1160, 1236
Alter, R., 0359
Althann, R., 0192, 0465
[Amado] Lévy-Valensi, E., 0957
Andersen, F.I., 1104, 1223
Andre, G., 0484
Ararat, N., 0667
Archer, G.L., 1073
Asensio, F., 0086
Astell, A., 0929
Atkinson, D., 1086, 1303
Aufrecht, W.E., 1121

Bachar, S., 0350
Baird, R.M., 0872
Bakan, D., 0965
Baker, A., 0206
Baker, J.A., 0819
Baker, W.C., 1261
Bakon, S., 0789, 1359
Bardtke, H., 0772
Barge, L., 0611
Barnes, W.E., 0121
Barr, J., 0039, 0896, 0900, 1375
Barré, M.L., 0215
Barron, M.C., 0470
Baruani, B., 0877
Baskin, J.R., 0704, 0727
Batten, L.W., 0448
Beauchamp, É., 0214

Bechtel, L., 0749a, 1368
Beck, H.F., 1022
Becker, E.L., 0884
Beeby, H.D., 0295
Beer, G., 0108
Begg, C.T., 0572
Benamozegh, E., 0463, 0776
Bennett, T.M., 0887, 1058, 1173, 1271
Berg, W., 0087, 0521
Bergant, D., 0438, 0468, 0564, 0628, 0837, 0936, 1232
Berges, U., 0018, 1013
Berry, D.L., 0813
Besserman, L.L., 0712
Beuken, W.A.M., 0071, 0091, 0110, 1392
Bezuidenhout, L.C., 0072, 0401
Blackwood, A., 1286
Blank, S.H., 0076, 0282
Blei, K., 1225
Bloch, E., 0537
Blommerde, A., 0902
Blumenthal, D.R., 0190
Blumenthal, E., 0068, 0598
Boadt, L., 0897
Bogert, E.A., 1019
Böhles, M., 0642
Bonnard, P.E., 0536
Bonora, A., 0540, 1083
Borger, R., 0404, 1114
Borgonovo, G., 0843, 0931
Böswald, R., 1278
Bowes, P.J., 1043
Brandle, W., 1148
Brandon, S.G.F., 0964, 0967
Brates (Cavero), L., 0754
Bräumer, H., 1255
Breitbart, S., 1350
Brenner, A., 0012, 0355, 0562
Breytenbach, A.P.B., 0764
Brim, C., 0534

Brin, G., 0101
Brinker, M., 0845
Brown, M.W., 0533
Brown, W.E., 1004
Brownlee, W.H., 1115
Brüning, C., 0383a
Bruston, C., 0207
Burden, J.J., 0804, 0841
Burns, J.B., 0106, 0107, 0181, 0182, 0184, 0239, 0492
Burrows, M., 0335
Buttenwieser, M., 1203

Caesar, L.O., 0829
Calati, B., 0568
Calvin, J., 0753
Camhy, O., 0483, 0496
Cañellas, G., 1097
Caquot, A., 0419, 1105
Carlisle, T.J., 1224
Carpentier, J-M., 0732
Carson, D.A., 0370, 0662
Carstensen, R.N., 0296, 0737
Cepeda Calzada, P., 0506, 0778, 0779
Ceresko, A.R., 0268, 0279, 0494, 0874, 0903, 1382
Chbeir, T., 0090
Cheney, M., 0576, 0688, 0809, 0831
Chiegegatti, A., 1027, 1308
Chin, C., 0157, 0164
Chiolerio, M., 0069
Christensen, D., 0558, 0766
Christo, G.E., 0198
Ciccarese, M.P., 0092, 0709
Cimosa, M., 0454, 0994
Ciuba, E., 0690
Clark, D.J., 0251
Clines, D.J.A., 0010, 0025, 0057, 0095, 0099, 0100, 0201, 0513, 0835, 1250, 1347, 1348, 1365, 1369
Coggi, R., 0466, 0717
Collins, B., 0958, 1185
Collins, J.J., 1130

Conte, G., 1379
Coogan, M.D., 0015
Cook, A., 0505
Cook, J., 0255
Cooper, A., 0008, 0028, 0861
Corey, L., 1080
Cornelius, I., 0397, 0600, 0760
Cotter, D., 0089
Couroyer, B., 0412, 0424
Course, J.E., 0061, 0982
Cowe, S.P., 0334
Cox, C., 0067, 0109, 0272, 0995
Cox, D., 0056, 0059, 0063, 0269, 0914, 1046, 1283, 1304
Craigie, P.C., 0908, 1176
Crenshaw, J.L., 0105, 0137, 0390, 0481, 1354
Crossan, J.D., 1387
Crumbach, K.H., 0629
Crüsemann, F., 0498
Curtis, J.B., 0173, 0307, 0308, 0311, 0332, 0432, 0485, 0741, 0773

Dahood, M., 0096, 0126, 0277, 0321, 0326, 0402, 0405, 0422, 0794, 0893, 0901, 0907
Dailey, T.F., 0392, 0408, 0437, 0446, 0509, 0573, 0578, 0687, 0830, 0854, 0930, 0974, 0975, 1025, 1166, 1167, 1189
Damico, A., 0716
Davies, J.A., 0159
Davis, E.F., 0487
Davis, M.V., 0881
Day, J., 0574
de Boer, P.A.H., 0445
de la Fuente, A., 0486
de Morr, J.C., 0910
de Pury, R., 0546
de Regt, L.J., 0151, 0171, 0983, 0984
de Rouville, O., 1338
de Wilde, A., 0237, 0431, 1222, 1231
De Gugliemo, A., 0161

Dedmon, R., 0547
Deiter, J., 0707
Delcor, M., 1127
Dell, K.J., 0683
Deselaers, P., 0696, 1293
Dhorme, E.P., 1211
Diaz, J.S., 1236
di Nola, A.M., 1319
Dick, M.B., 0263, 0286, 0287, 0288
Dietrich, L.J., 1024
Diewert, D., 0127, 0310, 0328
DiLella, A., 1339
Dion, P.E., 0803, 1009
Dittrich, W.F., 1087, 1351
Dobson, J.H., 0790, 1192
Doignon, J. 0705
Donald, T., 1168
Doniach, W.S., 0121
Dornisch, L., 0916, 1334
Driver, G.R., 0103, 0406, 0890, 0892
Driver, S.R., 1202
Duquoc, C., 1388
Durand, J., 0758

Eaton, J.H., 1237
Ebach, J., 0203, 1341
Edwards, C., 0923
Eerdmans, B.D., 1259
Ehrlich, E.L., 0742
Eising, H., 0469
Ellison, H.L., 1272
Epp, T.H., 1263
Erikson, G., 0013, 0681, 1049
Ewing, W.B., 1276

Fadeji, S.O., 0352
Faur, J., 0634
Fedrizzi, P., 1218
Feinberg, C.L., 0905, 1028
Fernandez M.N., 0998
Ferreiro, A., 0714
Festorazzi, F., 0500
Feuer, L.S., 0920

Fisch, H., 0680, 0832
Fishbane, M., 0075, 0488, 0613, 0762
Fisher, L.R., 0221
Fitzmyer, J.A., 1106
Fleming, D.E., 0031, 0664
Floristan, C. 1388
Fohrer, G., 0011, 0285, 0294, 0338, 0473, 0670, 0799, 0812, 1029, 1209, 1294, 1389
Fontaine, C.R., 0113, 0590, 0684, 1047
Fontaine, J., 0706
Ford, L.S., 0353
Forrest, R.W.E., 0451, 0560, 0615, 0838
Fox, M.V., 0384
Francisco, C.T., 0888
Francisco, N.A., 0608
François, F., 0357
Freedman, D.N., 0062, 0297, 0894, 1343
Freund, Y., 0456, 0516
Fronius, H., 1230
Frost, G.E., 1279
Frye, J.B., 0765, 0791, 0797
Fuchs, G., 0508, 0603, 0860
Fullerton, K., 0085, 0133, 0134, 0409, 0447

Galling, K., 0188
Gammie, J.G., 0414, 0580, 0992, 0996
Garcia C.M., 0186, 0187, 0460, 0461
García, F., 1113
García-Morena, A., 0973, 1084
Gard, D.H., 0462
Garland, D.D., 1273
Garrett, S.R., 1137
Gaster, T.H., 0228
Gavaler, C.P., 0569
Gelber, S.M., 1377
Geller, S.A., 0252
Gemuyt, F., 0474
Gentry, P.J., 0999
Gerber, I.J., 0784
Gerritsen, A., 0949
Gese, H., 1003

Geyer, C-F., 0867
Geyer, J.B., 0240
Gibbs, P.T., 1171
Gibson, J.C.L., 0426, 0647, 0875, 0913, 1238
Gilkey, L., 0788, 1018, 1162
Gillischewski, E., 0084
Gilpin, W.C., 1390
Ginsberg, H.L., 0539, 1320
Girard, R., 0552, 0553, 0570
Gitay, Z., 0048a, 0585b, 0760a
Gladson, J., 0646
Glatzer, N.N., 0740, 1374, 1385
Goldschmidt, H.L., 0541, 0738
Good, E.M., 0651, 0817, 1247, 1253
Goodheart, E., 1006
Gordis, R., 0020, 0235, 0339, 0423, 0425, 0621, 0655, 1172, 1220, 1226, 1260
Gorea, M., 0124
Görg, M., 0023, 0034
Gorringe, T.J., 0868
Gosling, F., 0806
Gowan, D.E., 0362, 0685
Grabbe, L.L., 0898
Gradl, F., 0420
Gramlich, M.L., 0542
Gray, G.B., 0814, 1202
Gray, J., 0592, 0989, 1107, 1194
Grayston, K., 0029, 0584
Green, B., 1360
Greenberg, M., 0718, 0825, 1196
Greenfield, J.C., 1196
Greenhalgh, S., 0626
Greenstein, E., 0383b
Grelot, P., 0407
Gross, C.D., 0176
Gross, H., 0246, 1242
Guillaume, A., 1005, 1265
Guillaumin, M-L., 0703
Guinan, M.D., 1243
Gustafson, J.M., 1355
Gutiérrez, G., 1078

Haag, H., 0691
Habel, N., 0304, 0471, 0512, 0524, 0862, 0883, 1178, 1239
Hagedorn, U., 0707, 0710
Halpern, B., 0783
Han, J.H., 0365, 0978
Handy, L.K., 0030, 0527, 0585, 0909
Hanson, A.T., 0722, 0744, 1217
Haplern, B., 0168
Häring, H., 1067
Harris, R.L., 0692
Harris, S.L., 0264, 0620, 1179
Harrison, G., 0851
Harrop, G.C., 0430
Hartley, J.E., 0852, 1248
Hay, D.M., 0870
Heater, H., 0991, 1197
Heckelman, J., 0786, 1344
Hedinger, U., 0940
Heinen, K., 1229, 1249
Hemraj, S., 0301
Hengstenberg, E.W., 1325
Hermisson, H-J., 0245a, 1381
Herrmann, W., 0428
Herz, N., 0138, 0399
Hess, J.-J., 0139, 0400
Hesse, F., 1227
Hill, R.C., 0256
Hirsh, N.D., 1032
Höffken, P., 1336
Hoffman, R., 0006, 0769
Hoffman, Y., 0602, 0844, 1039
Hoffmann, G., 0170
Holbert, J.C., 0223, 0270, 0850
Holland, J.A., 0674
Holm-Nielsen, S., 0575, 0785a
Holman, J., 0218
Holmgrew, F., 0495
Hölscher, G., 0210
Horne, M.P., 1143
Horst, F., 1212
Houtman, C., 0050
Huberman-Scholnick, S., 0363, 0780, 0785

Hudal, A., 0209
Hulme, W., 0873, 0876, 1213
Hunter, A.G., 1356
Hurvitz, A., 0003
Hyman, F.C., 1091

Inch, M., 1287
Irwin, W.A., 0131, 0189
Israel, S., 0538, 0605

Jacob, B., 0037, 0043, 0044, 0049, 0125,
    0129, 0148, 0153, 0160, 0177
Jacobs, I., 0724, 1128
Jacobsen, T., 0070
Jacobson, R., 1335
Jakubiec, C., 0343
Jamieson-Drake, D.W., 0395
Janzen, J.G., 0128, 0528, 0623, 0774,
    0971, 1240
Jason, H., 0543
Jeremias, J., 0561
Job, J.B., 1280, 1289
Johns, D.A., 0303
Johnson, L.D., 1274
Jones, E., 1262
Jongeling, B., 1100, 1108, 1109
Jonasson, K., 0013, 0681, 1049
Joosten, J., 0770, 0775, 1054
Joüon, P., 0038, 0146, 0163, 0262, 0276
Jung, C.G., 0946

Kahn, J.H., 0942, 1062
Kaiser, O., 0452, 1155
Kamnengiesser, C., 1326
Kaplan, L.J., 0440
Kapusta, M.A., 0945
Katz, Robert L., 0079, 0939
Kaufman, S.A., 1101
Kaufmann, U.M., 0750
Kautz, J.R., 0266
Kautzsch, K., 0001
Kee, H.C., 1131
Keel, O., 0348, 0356, 0375

Kegler, J., 0378
Kelley, P.H., 0052
Kelly, B.H., 0222, 0225
Kent, H.H., 1266
Kessler, R., 0217
Kimhi, M., 0728
Kinet, D., 0522, 0579, 1378
King, H.M., 1267
Kinner W.J.V., 0413
Kisch, J., 0518, 0955
Kissane, E., 1031, 1204
Klein, J.P., 0768
Klein, L., 1370
Knauf, E.A., 0228
Knibb, M.A., 1134
Knight, H., 1151
Koops, R., 0979
Kubina, V., 0351, 1074
Kuhl, C., 1372, 1373
Kuhm, H., 0280
Kuhn, J., 1284
Kurzweil, B., 0673
Kusenberg, H., 0895
Kushner, H.S., 1093
Kutsch, E., 0193, 0197, 0202, 0519, 1059
Kuyper, L.J., 0429

Lacocque, A., 0644, 0666, 0915, 0917
Laeuchli, S., 0591, 1366
Lafont, G., 0645
Laks, H.J., 0721, 0746
Lamb, J., 0749, 1098
Lang, B., 0354
Langenhorst, G., 0833
Larcher, C., 1206
Larue, G., 1153
Laserson, M., 0777, 0911
Lasine, S., 0612, 0787
Laurin, R., 1033
Lavoie, J-J., 1383
Lee, P., 0872a, 1098a
Leibowitz, J., 0725
Leloir, L., 0035, 0743, 0751

Lerner, B.D., 0827, 0863
Lesses, R., 0459
Levenson, J.D., 1275
Lévêque, J., 0267, 0379, 0514, 0624, 0753, 0822, 1020, 1063, 1066, 1190, 1269, 1296, 1326
Levin, S., 0581
Levine, B., 0554
Levinger, J., 0726
Levoratti, A.J., 1164, 1361
Lichtenstein, A., 0820, 0846
Lillie, W., 0336
Lipinksi, E., 0800, 0899
Littleton, M.R., 0515
Loader, J.A., 0374, 0391, 0497, 0625, 0781, 1337
Loades, A.L., 0918
Lobato Fernández, J.B., 1256
Löhr, M., 0130, 0178
Long, T.G., 1345
Long, T.J., 0631
Loretz, O., 0064, 0174, 0238
Loyd, D.E., 0976
Luebering, C., 1026a
Lundberg, M.J., 0382
Lust, J., 0094

Maag, V., 0009, 1291
Maas, J., 0954
Macbeath, A., 1264
MacKenzie, R.A.F., 0337, 0544, 0970, 1214, 1251
Maggioni, B., 0501
Maia, P.A., 0869
Maillot, A., 0815, 0969, 1158
Malchow, B.V., 0274, 0386, 0619
Mangan, C., 1123, 1124
Manni, M.A., 0165
Many, G., 0848
Manzanedo, M.F., 0713, 0919
Marböck, J., 1290
Marnewick, J.C., 0764
Marqusee, M., 0756

Martin, G.W., 0229, 0299
Martínez, J.M., 1233
Martini, C.M., 1085, 1299
Mason, M., 0650
Mastin, B.A., 1120
Maston, T.B., 0637
Matheney, M.P., 1321
Mathew, G., 0453a
Matthews, M.S., 0747
Mattingly, G.L., 0601, 1144
Mattioli, A., 0641, 1015, 1064
McCabe, R.V., 0305
McCormick, S., 0051
McDonagh, K., 0491
McKay, J.W., 0300
McKeating, H., 1318
McKechnie, J., 0531
McKenna, D.L., 1244
McKibben, B., 0380, 0627
Meier, S., 0027, 0767
Meiron, M., 0372
Mende, T., 0216, 0309, 1258
Mers, M., 0117
Mettinger, T.N.D., 0525, 0700, 0763
Michael, J.H., 0864
Michel, D., 0657
Michel, W.L., 0026, 0080, 0213, 0291, 0302, 0630, 0856, 0904, 0906
Miles, J.A., 0818
Milgrom, J., 1000
Millard, A.R., 0114
Millard, M., 1362
Miller, J.E., 0088, 0389
Miller, W.S., 0559, 1050
Mintingh, L.M., 0464
Mitchell, C., 1017
Mitchell, S., 1195, 1198
Möller, M., 0616
Mooney, E.F., 0927
Moore, M.S., 0807, 1092
Moore, R.D., 0548
Moretto, G., 0924
Morgan, G., 0865

Morre, R.D., 0065
Morrow, F.J., 1102
Morrow, W., 0442
Mowinckel, S., 0185
Muenchow, C., 0443
Müller, H-P., 0005, 0366, 0385, 0416, 0595, 0596, 0604, 0972, 1147, 1270, 1376
Mulrooney, J., 0260, 1191
Muraoka, T., 1116
Murphy, R.E., 0882, 1281
Murray, G., 0606
Murtagh, J., 0586

Nakazawa, K., 0450
Nash, J., 0549
Nash, R.T., 0649
Negoiță, A., 0593
Neher, A., 0535
Neiman, D., 1193
Nel, P.J., 0373, 0507
Nemo, P., 0643
Neri, P., 1349
Newell, B.L., 0433
Newsom, C.A., 0381, 0503, 0639, 0933, 1012, 1363
Niccacci, A., 0250, 0333
Nicholls, P.H., 1044
Nicholson, E.W., 1150
Nielsen, E., 0523
Nielsen, K., 0017, 0583
Nimmo, P.W., 0879, 0962
Noegel, S.B., 0122a, 0129a, 0810, 0811

O'Connor, Daniel J., 0361, 0441, 0457, 0555, 0563, 0588, 0950, 1142
O'Connor, Donal, 0520a, 0530a, 0585c
O'Connor, K.M., 0074
Oberforcher, R., 0478, 0490
Odell, D., 0403
Oeming, M., 0289, 0290, 0640, 0771
Oosthuizen, M.J., 0016
Or-Bach, I., 0963

Orlinsky, H.M., 0167
Ortiz de Urtaran, F., 0275, 0556
Orwall, L., 1184
Osswald, E., 0284, 0635
Owen, G.F., 0033
Owens, J.J., 0002

Pace, U., 0997
Pardee, D., 0224
Parsons, G.W., 0824, 0839, 0886, 1040
Patrick, D., 0439, 0934, 0935
Paul, S.M., 0141, 0504
Paul, S.M., 0097
Payne, J.B., 1327
Peake, A.S., 1315, 1340
Pellauer, D., 0385
Penar, T., 0195
Penchansky, D., 0828, 1300
Penzenstadler, J., 0889
Perani, M., 0632, 0719, 0801, 1177
Perdue, L.G., 0066, 0073, 0111, 0136, 0622, 0853, 1161, 1188, 1390
Perraymond, M., 0759
Petersen, M., 0261
Pifano, P., 0472
Pipes, B.R., 1070
Pixley, J.V., 1156, 1157, 1234
Plank, K.A., 1180
Pleins, J.D., 0702, 1094
Polzin, R., 0004, 1034, 1386
Pope, M.H., 0144, 1221, 1311
Porter, S.E., 0458
Potter, H., 1352
Potter, R., 1216
Prado, J., 0212
Pretorius, P.A.C., 1026
Preuß, H.D., 0345, 0594
Priest, J., 0610, 0698, 0912
Pyper, H., 0453, 1357

Quillo, R., 0959, 1053

Raabe, P.R., 1082

Radinowicz, M.A., 0826
Rahman, Y., 0582
Rahnenführer, D., 1129
Raine, K.J., 0757
Rao, S.P., 0022, 0587
Raphael, D.D., 0671, 0966
Ratner, R., 0194
Rauchwarger, J., 0545
Raurell, F., 0638, 0694, 1141, 1367
Ravasi, G., 0648, 0697, 1023, 1254, 1295
Redditt, P.L., 0231
Reddy, M.P., 1036
Reid, S.A., 0941
Reider, J., 0147
Reiser, W., 0566
Reiterer, F.V., 0482
Remus, M., 0476
Rendsburg, G., 0077
Reventlow, H.G., 0241, 0711
Rexroth, K., 1316
Reyburn, W., 1200
Reynierse, J.H., 0943, 0944
Ricciotti, G., 0042
Riebl, M., 0755
Riggans, W., 0115, 0116
Riley, W., 0701
Rimbach, J.A., 0098
Rinaldi, G., 0036
Ritter, P., 0393
Roberts, J.J.M., 0135, 0247, 0849, 0968
Robertson, D., 0502, 1330, 1386
Rodd, C., 1252, 1380a
Rohr, R., 1082a
Ronen, M., 0925, 0980
Rongy, H., 0019
Rosenberg, D.W., 1282
Ross, J.F., 0322
Rottenberg, M., 0047
Rouillard, H., 0323
Rowley, H.H., 1245, 1312
Rowold, H.J., 0346, 0387, 0427, 0617
Roy, A., 0960
Rubenstein, R.L., 1007

Ruckman, P.S., 1285
Ruíz, J-P., 0383, 1014
Ruprecht, E., 0411, 0782, 1065
Rutler, G.W., 1292

Sacchi, P., 0145
Safire, W., 0932, 1011, 1306
Samudi, J., 0169
Sánchez, B.G., 1088
Sanders, P.S., 1384
Sarna, N.M., 0021, 0162, 0179, 0811a, 0891, 1196
Sarrazin, B., 0367, 0847
Sawicki, M., 0347
Sawyer, J.F.A., 0821, 1037
Scafella, F., 1331
Scammon, J.H., 0660
Schaller, B., 0866, 0990, 1132, 1135, 1332
Schapiro, D.S., 1324
Scheffler, E., 0961
Schimmel, S., 0951, 1079
Schlafer, D.J., 0885
Schlobin, R.C., 0686
Schmidt, P., 0614, 0658, 1002
Schneider, T., 0396
Schreiner, S., 0479, 0729, 0752
Schreiner, S.E., 0715, 0734, 0735, 0736
Schubert, B., 0609
Schulweis, H.M., 0745
Schulz, K.A., 1089
Schwienhorst-Schönberger, L., 0014
Seidel, H., 1136
Seitz, C., 0871, 1051
Settlemire, C.C., 0249
Severino Croatto, J., 1159
Sewall, R.B., 1317
Sharma, A., 0591, 1366
Shapiro, D.S., 0477, 1324
Sheldon, M., 1068
Shelley, J.C., 0435
Sia, S., 0699
Silbermann, A., 1010
Silver, D.J., 0723

Simundson, D.J., 0520, 0878, 1246, 1358
Siwy, J.M., 0952
Skehan, P.W., 0119, 0122, 0265, 0319, 0320, 0329, 0340, 1030, 1314
Slotki, J.J., 0152
Smick, E.B., 0802, 0840, 0857, 0859, 0977, 1342
Smith, C.E., 0592
Smith, D.L., 0633
Smith, E.L., 1322
Smith, Gary V., 0093, 1163, 1187
Smith, W.C., 0273
Snaith, N.H., 0055, 0793, 1268
Snell, P., 0661
Sokoloff, M., 1110
Southwick, J., 0551
Spangenberg, I.J.J., 0421, 1095,
Speer, J., 0208
Speiser, E.A., 0511
Sperka, J.S., 1288
Spieckermann, H., 0529
Spittler, R.P., 1135a
Stamm, J.J., 0204, 0205, 1139
Stec, D.M., 0149, 1125, 1126
Stedman, R.C., 1071
Steinberg, M., 0532
Steinmann, A.E., 0808a, 0984a, 1055
Steinmann, J., 1057
Steins, G., 0014
Stier, F., 1205
Stockhammer, M., 0636, 1140
Stockhammer, S.E., 0654, 0659
Stockton, E., 0816
Strauß, H., 0530
Strauss, J.D., 1277
Strolz, W., 0656
Strong, D., 0987
Susman, M., 0739
Sutcliffe, E.F., 0112, 0118, 0120, 0132, 0154, 0196, 0219, 0292, 0324, 0325, 0330, 0331
Swanepoel, M.G., 0156
Szpek, H.M., 0123, 1201

Tai, N., 0872a, 1098a
Talstra, E., 0227
Tang, S.Y., 0283
Tate, M.E., 0298
Taylor, D.B., 1301, 1302
Taylor, W.S., 0938, 1152
Tengbom, M., 1069
Terrien, S., 0342, 0565, 0672, 0761, 1183, 1207, 1210
Thelen, M.F., 0467, 0607
Theobald, G., 1145, 1149, 1165
Thexton, C., 0236
Thomas, D., 1235
Thomason, B., 1099
Thompson, K., 1056
Tilley, T., 0369, 0434, 0668, 1146
Tomasoni, F., 0663, 0926
Tortolone, G.M., 0475, 0921
Townsend, T.P., 1016
Toynbee, A.J., 0855
Tsevat, M., 1313
Tsmudi, Y., 0368
Tur-Sinai, N.H., 1208
Turoldo, D.M., 1307

Ullendorff, E., 0078
Unsvåg, H.H., 0376, 0377
Urbrock, W.J., 0054, 0679, 0792, 0796
Urbrock, W.J., 0675

Vall, G., 0042a, 0398, 0808, 0842
van der Horst, P., 1133
van der Lugt, P., 0082, 0253, 0985, 1048
van der Zee, W.R., 0653
van Duin, K., 0078a
van Oorschot, J., 0257, 0364
van Praag, H., 0953, 1081
van Rensburg, J.F.J., 0083, 0805, 0981
van Selms, A., 0293, 0798, 1241
van Wolde, E.J., 0436, 0834
Vasholtz, R.I., 1117
Vawter, B., 0493
Vella, P., 0175

Vermeylen, J., 0371, 0652, 1297
Vincent, M., 0708
Vinton, P., 0489
Vischer, W., 0689, 1310
Viviers, H., 0318
Vogels, W., 0040, 0041, 0045, 0046, 0665,
    0947, 0948, 1021, 1038, 1041, 1045,
    1309
Vogler, T.A., 0748
von Orelli, A., 0858, 1328
von Rad, G., 0248, 1060, 1061, 1170
von Rohr Sauer, A., 1154
von Speyr, A., 1219

Waddle, S.H., 0081
Wagner, S., 0455, 0618, 1096
Wahl, H-M., 0232, 0312, 0313, 0314,
    0316, 0317, 1138
Waldman, N.M., 0032, 0394
Warner, M., 1181
Waterman, L., 0200
Watson, W., 0150
Webster, E., 0058, 0271
Weigart, M., 0344
Weimar, P., 0007, 0823
Weimer, J.D., 0795
Weinberg, J., 0480, 0731
Weinfeld, M., 0599
Weiser, A., 1215
Weiss, M., 0024
Weiss, R., 1111, 1112, 1118
West, G., 0048, 0585a, 1353
Westermann, C., 0550, 1035, 1042
Wharton, J.A., 1333
Whedbee, J.W., 0677
Whybray, R.N., 0499
Wiersbe, W.W., 1305
Wilcox, J.T., 0922
Wildberger, H., 0937
Willi-Plein, I., 0226, 0695
Williams, D.L., 0053
Williams, J.G., 0349, 0360, 0449, 0526,
    0928, 1090

Williams, R.J., 1380
Wilson, L., 0669
Winton-Thomas, D., 1174
Witte, M., 0233, 0234, 0244, 0315
Wittenberg, G.H., 0567, 0880, 1186
Wolfers, D., 0060, 0102, 0104, 0155, 0158,
    0172, 0180, 0191, 0230, 0242, 0243,
    0245, 0254, 0258, 0281, 0306, 0327,
    0417, 0418, 0557, 0571, 0577, 0986,
    1199, 1371, 1393
Wolters, A., 0444
Würthwein, E., 0341
Wyatt, N., 0183

Xella, P., 0140

Yaffe, M.D., 0716, 0720, 0730
Yamaga, T., 0278
Yancey, P., 1346
Yates, K.M., 1323
Yeager, J., 0509
York, A.D., 1103
Young, W.A., 0415

Zahrnt, H., 1072, 1076
Zenger, E., 1075, 1278
Zerafa, P., 1175
Ziegler, J., 0988, 0993
Zimmerman, F., 0142, 0410
Zimmermann, R., 0259
Zink, J.K., 0166, 0211, 1001
Zuck, R.B., 0199, 1228, 1391
Zuckerman, B., 1119, 1122, 1298, 1329
Zurro, E., 0143